Science Textbook
Year 3–4

Series Editor: Alan Jarvis

Wendy Hart
Diane Lowton
Heather Monaghan
Joan O'Sullivan
Judith Willis

WITHDRAWN

Letts

EDUCATIONAL

D1323847

Every effort has been made to trace copyright holders and to obtain their permission for the use of copyright material. The authors and publishers would gladly receive information enabling them to rectify any error or omission in subsequent editions.

Photographic credits
Robert Battersby/Bosun: pp.15 (top left), 41 (centre right), 52, 54, 60, 63, 68, 76, 96, 100 (bottom left, centre left, centre right, right), 111; John Walmsley: p.15 (top right); Dr P Marazzi/Science Photo Library: p.15 (bottom); Science Photo Library: p.19 (top and bottom); Richard Powers/Life File: p.40 (top); Paul Seheult/Eye Ubiquitous: p.40 (bottom); Julia Waterlow/Eye Ubiquitous: p.41 (top); Ecoscene/Angela Hampton: p.41 (centre left); Aubrey J Slaughter/Life File: p.41 (bottom); Allan Morton/Science Photo Library: p.108; John Sanford/Science Photo Library: p.109 (top); NASA/Science Photo Library: p.109 (bottom); Ecoscene: p.113 (top); O Svyatoslavsky/Life File: p.113 (bottom).

First published 1998

Reprinted 1998

Letts Educational, Schools and Colleges Division,
9–15 Aldine Street, London W12 8AW
Tel: 0181 740 2270
Fax: 0181 740 2280

Text © Wendy Hart, Alan Jarvis, Diane Lowton, Heather Monaghan, Joan O'Sullivan, Judith Willis

Designed, edited and produced by Gecko Limited, Bicester, Oxon

Illustrations by Sally Artz, Sarah John, Margaret Jones, John Plumb, Dave Poole and Chris Rothero

Picture research by Lodestone Publishing Ltd

All our rights reserved. No part of this publication may be reproduced, stored in a retrieval system, or transmitted, in any form or by any means, electronic, mechanical, photocopying, recording or otherwise, without prior permission of Letts Educational.

British Library Cataloguing-in-Publication Data
A CIP record for this book is available from the British Library

ISBN 1 84085 061 2

Printed in Great Britain by Clowes Group Ltd

Letts Educational is the trading name of BPP [Letts Educational] Ltd

Contents

How do I get the best out of this book?   5

Humans and other animals   9
Living animals   10
Food and feeding   12
Teeth   14
Exercise   16
Bones   18
Growing and changing   20
Test your knowledge   22

Living things   23
Plants   24
Seed dispersal   26
Growing plants   28
Designed to survive   30
A place to live   32
Living together   34
Test your knowledge   36

Materials and their properties   37
What things are made from   38
Where materials come from   40
Soil   42
Separating solids   44
Keeping things hot or cold   46
Solids, liquids and gases   48
Test your knowledge   50

Changes in materials   51
Mixing materials   52
Dissolving   54
Filtering   56
Evaporating   58
Thermometers   60
Melting and freezing   62
Test your knowledge   64

All about forces   65
What can forces do?   66
Gravity   68
Springs and elastic bands   70
Balanced and unbalanced forces   72
Floating and sinking   74
Magnetic forces   76
Test your knowledge   78

Light and sound   79
Learning about light   80
Shadows   82
Transparent, translucent and opaque   84
Sound vibrations   86
Sound can travel   88
Hearing sound   90
Test your knowledge   92

Electricity   93
Making a circuit   94
Batteries   96
Buzzers and motors   98
Switches   100
More circuits   102
Being safe with electricity   104
Test your knowledge   106

The Earth and beyond   107
The Earth, the Sun and the Moon   108
Movements of the Sun   110
Day and night   112
Shadows through the day   114
The seasons   116
The Moon   118
Test your knowledge   120

Glossary   121

How do I get the best out of this book?

How is the book organised?

The **contents page** near the front of the book shows you the topics in each chapter.

I look at the contents page to find where something is in the book.

Each chapter has a different colour to make it easier to find. For example, 'Humans and other animals' is blue.

There are **eight chapters** in the book. Each chapter is organised in the same way. They have:

- an **introduction page** – The top part of this page tells you what you should already know. Use this to check what you can remember about each topic. If there is something you don't know, you will have to do some catching up. The bottom part of the page shows you what you will learn in the chapter.
- **topics** – These are shown across two pages and tell you the science you need to learn.
- a **'Test your knowledge' page** at the end of each chapter – This has interesting questions to test what you have learnt.

At the end of the book there is a **glossary**. This has important science words for each chapter and tells you what they mean. These words are shown in **bold** on the topic pages.

Before I start a new topic I look at the first page of the chapter. This helps me to think about what I need to know before I start a topic.

If I am not sure what a bold word means on a topic page I look it up in the glossary or ask my teacher.

How do I use the topic pages?

Each topic is shown across two pages and is set out in the same way.

The summary tells me the key things I need to learn and understand in the topic.

The words and pictures help me to learn more about science. I need to be able to describe science using my own words and pictures to tell others what I mean.

Bold words are science words I need to learn and use in my own science work. I can look most of them up in the glossary if I am not sure what they mean.

Soil

Soil is made when rocks are worn down. It is made of **particles** of different sizes. **Clay** particles are very fine and get sticky when they are wet. **Chalk** particles are also fine but do not become sticky when wet. **Sand** particles are bigger and gritty.

Looking at soil

Jack got some **soil** from his garden. He used a hand lens to look at it closely. He saw that the **particles** were different sizes, shapes and colours. He put the soil in a bottle with some water and shook it. At first it was cloudy. The next day he could see different layers.

▲ Soil and water shaken together.

▲ Soil and water once they have settled.

water
chalk
clay
sand
gravel

Jack went to stay with his grandfather. He wanted to see if the soil there was the same as in his own garden. Jack found that the thickness of each layer was different from his soil. His grandfather's soil had a thinner layer of **sand** and more **clay** and **chalk** than Jack's soil.

water
chalk
clay
sand
gravel

▲ Jack's soil sample.

▲ Grandfather's soil sample.

42

Many drawings have captions and labels. These help me to understand the pictures. I need to draw and label my own drawings like the ones in the book.

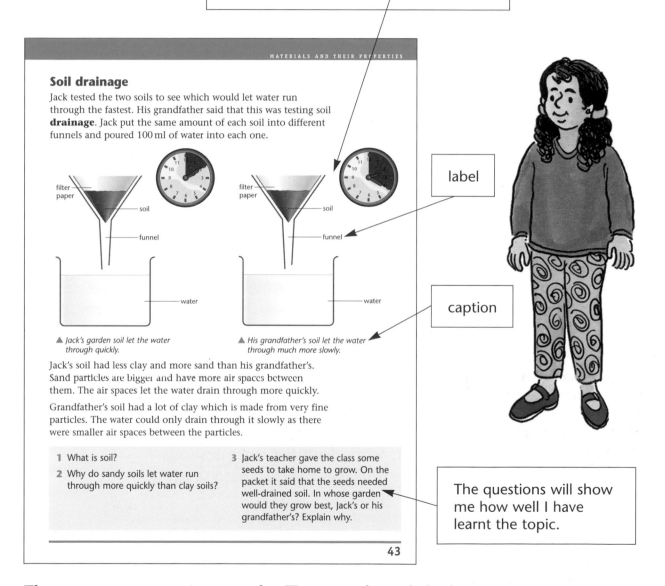

Soil drainage

Jack tested the two soils to see which would let water run through the fastest. His grandfather said that this was testing soil **drainage**. Jack put the same amount of each soil into different funnels and poured 100 ml of water into each one.

filter paper — soil — funnel — water

filter paper — soil — funnel — water

▲ Jack's garden soil let the water through quickly.

▲ His grandfather's soil let the water through much more slowly.

Jack's soil had less clay and more sand than his grandfather's. Sand particles are bigger and have more air spaces between them. The air spaces let the water drain through more quickly.

Grandfather's soil had a lot of clay which is made from very fine particles. The water could only drain through it slowly as there were smaller air spaces between the particles.

1 What is soil?

2 Why do sandy soils let water run through more quickly than clay soils?

3 Jack's teacher gave the class some seeds to take home to grow. On the packet it said that the seeds needed well-drained soil. In whose garden would they grow best, Jack's or his grandfather's? Explain why.

43

label

caption

The questions will show me how well I have learnt the topic.

There are more questions on the 'Test your knowledge' page at the end of each chapter. These will test how well you have understood the science you have learnt.

Things to remember

- **Read the words carefully.** You might not understand everything the first time you read it. Read each sentence slowly a few times. Then it should make more sense. If it doesn't, then ask your teacher what it means.

- It is important to make sure you **spell words the right way**. The words you must learn to spell are written in **bold** letters. Try to learn these words and use them in your own science work.

- **Learn the science facts** and try to understand the **science ideas**. These explain why things happen. Try to use these facts and ideas in your own science writing. You need to explain things clearly so that other people can understand.

- **Answer the questions well**. Always write in full sentences. Spell each word correctly. Always try to use the right science words in your answer. Use the words and pictures on the topic pages to help you work out what you need to say. Check your answer and try to make it better.

- **Use the correct ways of writing and drawing**. Make sure that you use the right units and symbols. Always label drawings clearly and properly.

- **Set your work out properly**. Follow the rules your teacher has told you for setting out your work. Number the questions in the right order. Cross out any mistakes neatly. Space your work sensibly on the page.

Humans and other animals

Before you start you should know that:
- humans and other animals are living things;
- humans need food and water to stay alive;
- taking exercise and eating the right food helps you to stay healthy;
- humans can see, hear, smell, taste and touch things;
- all people are alike in some ways but each person is different.

In this unit you will learn:
- how animals are alike;
- how animals are different;
- how animals and plants are linked together by the food they eat;
- that the shape of animals' teeth helps them to eat their special food;
- what happens to your body when you exercise;
- how bones help you to stand up and move;
- how people change as they grow up and get old;
- about life cycles.

Living animals

Living things are sorted into two groups, **animals** and **plants**.
All animals need food, and they all grow and move. They also
reproduce and get rid of waste from their bodies. Animals can
be divided into different groups such as birds, fish and insects.
The animals in each group are alike in some ways.

All sorts of animals

▼ *All of these living things are called **animals**.*

fish

bird

bee

human

snail

cat

All animals are alike in some ways.

All animals grow.

All animals eat. They need food.

All animals move.

All animals can have young ones – they **reproduce**.

How are animals put into groups?

Animals are sorted or classified into different groups.
Birds, **mammals**, **insects** and **fish** are some of the groups.

All animals in a group are the same in some ways but they also have some differences.

▼ *These are birds.*

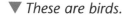

They both have wings.
They both lay eggs.

▼ *These are insects.*

They both have three body parts.
They both have six legs.

▼ *These are fish.*

They both have gills.
They both have fins.

▼ *These are mammals.*

They both have live babies.
The mothers make milk to feed their babies.

1 Write down the names of the two big groups of living things.

2 List four things that all animals can do.

Begin your sentence 'All animals can ...'

3 Which group do each of these animals belong to?

Write your answers in sentences.

goldfish

dragonfly

thrush

dog

Food and feeding

Plants and animals are linked together through food. Green plants can make their own food by using energy from the Sun. Some animals get their food by eating plants. Some animals eat other animals. All the food humans eat, once came from plants.

How do plants feed?

Plants make their own food. They are called **producers** because they can use energy from the Sun to grow.

All these are plants.

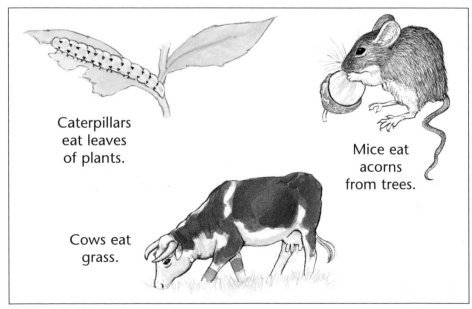

Caterpillars eat leaves of plants.

Mice eat acorns from trees.

Cows eat grass.

All animals eat. They need food to stay alive.

Some animals only eat plants. They are called **herbivores**.

Owls eat mice.

Spiders eat flies.

Cats eat birds.

Animals which eat meat are called **carnivores**.

Animals which eat other animals are called **predators**.

The animals they eat are called their **prey**.

What about human food?

Michelle has a meal of lamb chops, baked beans and chips.

Michelle is an **omnivore** because she eats both plants and meat.
Chips are made from potatoes.
Beans and tomatoes make baked beans.
Grass is eaten by lambs, and lamb chops come from lambs.
She would have no food without plants.

1 Find a plant, a herbivore and a carnivore in the pictures.
   Write your answers like this –
   'A squirrel is a ....
   because ....'

2 Choose a word from the box to finish each sentence.
   Spiders eat ....   Mice eat ....
   Cows eat ....   Cats eat ....

   | birds grass |
   | acorns flies |

3 Which animal is a predator of flies?

4 Daniel has a meal of chicken curry, lentil dahl and rice.
   Explain how it all comes from plants.

Teeth

Many animals need teeth so they can eat their food. Teeth are different shapes to suit the type of food each animal eats. Human babies are usually born without teeth. Then humans grow two sets of teeth during their lives. If you eat too many sugary foods and do not clean your teeth they can **decay**.

We need teeth to eat food

Look at the teeth of these animals.
They help the animals to eat their different foods.

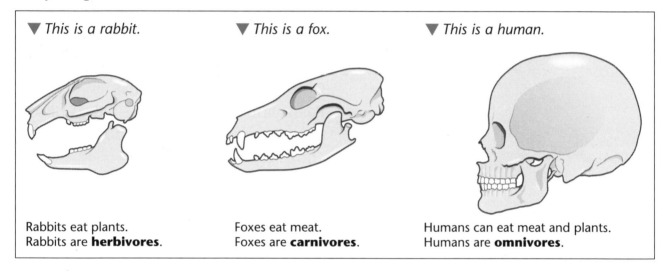

▼ *This is a rabbit.*

▼ *This is a fox.*

▼ *This is a human.*

Rabbits eat plants.
Rabbits are **herbivores**.

Foxes eat meat.
Foxes are **carnivores**.

Humans can eat meat and plants.
Humans are **omnivores**.

Humans also have teeth of different shapes. Each kind of tooth does a different job. Look at your teeth. Can you see the different shapes?

Incisors are sharp, for biting food.

Canines are pointed, for holding and tearing.

Molars have flat tops for grinding.

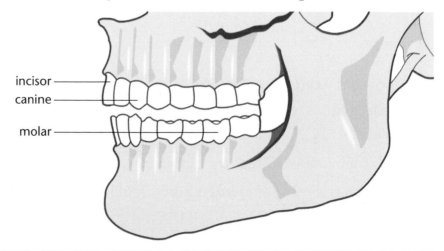

incisor

canine

molar

What happens to our teeth?

Most human babies are born without teeth. Babies do not need teeth because they drink milk and eat soft foods. They do not need to bite and chew.

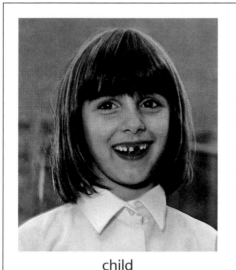

child

Young children grow a set of 20 teeth. These are called **milk teeth**. These teeth fall out when **permanent teeth** grow. Adults have a set of 32 permanent teeth.

adult

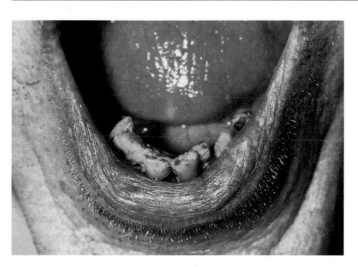

Teeth can decay if you:
- eat too many sticky sugary foods;
- do not clean your teeth regularly.

1 Finish the sentences by writing down what kind of food each of these animals eats.
   a Rabbits and sheep eat ....
   b Foxes eat ....
   c Humans eat ....

2 Name the teeth which are especially shaped for each of the following:
   a grinding food   c tearing food
   b biting food

3 Write down two things you can do to stop your teeth decaying.

Exercise

Your body changes when you exercise. When you rest your body soon gets back to normal. You can move because you have **muscles** connected to your bones. You use energy to move these muscles. Some things you do use very little energy. Some things use much more energy.

What happens when you exercise?

Your body changes in many ways.

▲ This is Jack. He gets a lot of exercise playing football.

▲ He uses energy to run and kick the ball.

▲ He breathes faster.

▲ His heart beats faster.

▲ He gets hot and sweaty.

▲ Then he rests.

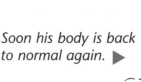

Soon his body is back to normal again. ▶

Understanding your body

Everyone has **muscles** connected to **bones**. You need muscles to move.

If you move your arms and legs slowly you can feel your muscles move.

You use up energy to move these muscles.

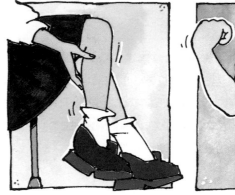

▼ *Some movements use very little energy.*

You breathe gently.
Your heart beats normally.
You do not get hot.

▼ *Some movements use lots of energy.*

You breathe quickly.
Your heart beats fast.
You get hot and sweaty.

The sweat is wet on your skin so it helps to cool you down just after exercise.

If you rest, your body soon gets back to normal.

1 Write down some things you do that use very little energy.

2 Write down some things you like to do that use lots of energy.

3 Explain how your body changes when you exercise.

4 Explain what happens to your body when you rest after exercise.

Bones

Humans have **skeletons** made of **bones**. The skeleton holds the body up and allows it to move. The bones are fitted together by **joints** which allow different amounts of movement. Examples of these joints are **hinge joints**, **ball and socket joints** and **sliding joints**.

Your skeleton

You have a **skeleton** inside your body. It is made of **bones**. It helps you to stand up and to move.

Without a skeleton you would just be a blob on the floor.

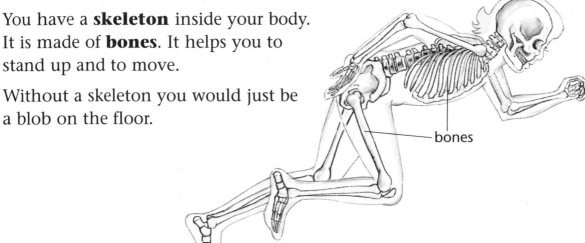

bones

How your leg moves

You can move because your bones are joined together.

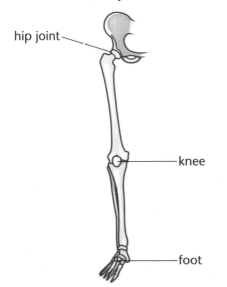

hip joint

knee

foot

Bend your knee joint.
It is a **hinge joint**.
You can bend it only one way.

Move your leg at your hip joint.
It is a **ball and socket joint**.
You can move it in any direction.

How your hand moves

Look at your hand.

How many joints can you find in your fingers?

Which way can they move? These are hinge joints too.

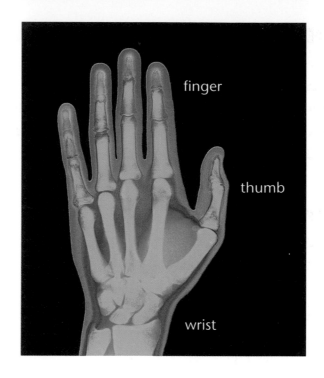

How your back moves

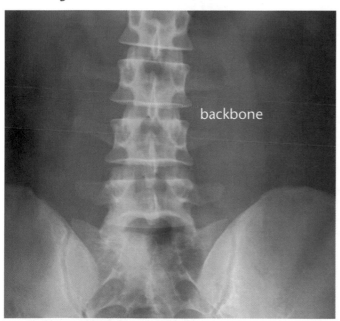

Some parts of your body have lots of little bones.

Look at your **wrist** and at the **backbone** in the pictures. These little bones slide against each other so you can bend and twist your body. They are **sliding joints**.

1 Explain why you need a skeleton.

2 Write two sentences describing where the joints are in your leg and in your arm.

3 Name three different kinds of joint and say where each one is.

Growing and changing

As humans grow they change. Babies change to become toddlers. As they get older they become adults. Adults are able to have babies of their own. This is known as a **life cycle**. Adults change as they grow older and at the end of their life they die.

Growing up

Humans start their lives when they are born. They change as they grow up and get older. They look different and they can do different things.

This is Yasmin when she was a baby. She had to be looked after all the time. How do babies need to be looked after?

This is Yasmin now she is eight. She can do lots of things for herself. What can you do now that you could not do when you were a baby?

This is Yasmin's sister. Do you think she is younger or older than Yasmin? Why do you think that?

Here is Yasmin's oldest sister and her husband. She is grown up. She has a baby.

Here is Yasmin's granny. She is an old lady now. Her husband has died. Yasmin helps to look after her.

Life cycles

A **life cycle** is a way of showing how animals grow from babies to adults who can have babies of their own. This starts the cycle all over again.

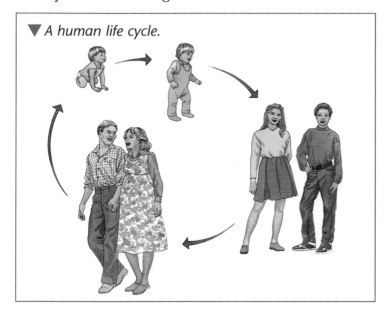
▼ A human life cycle.

Some animals like these have babies that look very like the adults as soon as they are born.

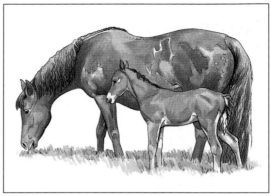

Some animals that lay eggs look very different as they go through the stages of their life cycle.

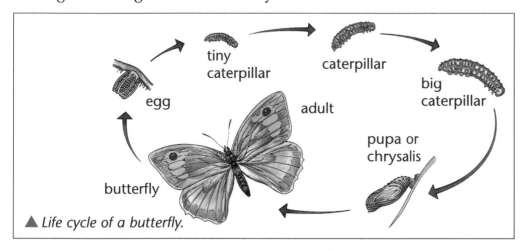
▲ Life cycle of a butterfly.

1 Write sentences which explain how human babies change as they grow up.

2 Draw a butterfly's egg and what comes out of it.

3 Draw a chrysalis and what it grows into.

Test your knowledge

1 Find the odd one out and then finish the sentence.

**wasp   spaniel   buttercup
robin   cod   centipede**

The odd one out is ....
because ....

2 What am I?   What am I?
■ I have two wings   ■ I have wings
■ I have a beak   ■ I have two
                                         antennae
■ I have claws on   ■ I have six legs
  my feet
■ I have feathers   ■ I have three
                                         body parts
■ I lay eggs in   ■ I get nectar
  a nest   from flowers
  I am ....   I am ....

3 Draw arrows from the bottom line to the top line to find the right food for these animals. One has been done for you.

spider cow bird mouse squirrel snail

caterpillar acorn fly nut grass lettuce

4 Choose words from the box to finish the sentences.

A rabbit eats grass.
It is ....
A cat eats birds.
It is ....
Sara eats fish and chips.
She is ....

**an omnivore
a herbivore
a carnivore**

5 Put these words in order, to make a life cycle diagram for the butterfly.

**butterfly
chrysalis
caterpillar**

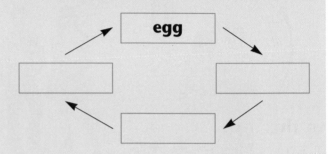

egg

6 Daniel is writing to his penfriend Jack, but some words are missing.

Copy the sentences, putting the words below in the spaces so Jack can understand the letter.

I get lots of .... playing football.

My heart .... fast and I get all

.... and .... but I have a

.... at half time and I soon get

back to ....

**beats   rest   exercise
normal   sweaty   hot**

Living things

Before you start you should know that:
- there are differences between things that are living and things that have never been alive;
- there are many kinds of plants and animals;
- different plants and animals live around your home and school;
- plants and animals live in places where they can find what they need.

In this unit you will learn:
- how all plants are alike;
- the names of different parts of a plant and what each part does;
- how seeds are spread around so new plants can grow;
- what seeds need to germinate and what plants need to grow;
- how some plants and animals are especially suited to the places where they live;
- that plants and animals living together need each other to survive.

Plants

Plants can be sorted into groups such as **mosses**, **ferns** and **flowering plants** like **trees**, **grasses** and **bushes**. All these plants use energy from the Sun to make food, grow and **reproduce**. They all have different parts. Each part of a plant does a particular job.

How can we group plants?

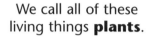

We call all of these living things **plants**.

trees

ferns

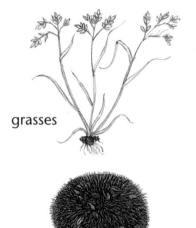

grasses

mosses

small plants

bushes

All these plants are alike in some ways. They also are different in some ways. We use these differences to sort them into groups.

What do all plants do?

Plants do not have to eat food like animals do.

All plants grow.

All green plants use energy from the Sun to make food.

All plants can make young ones (**reproduce**).

Parts of a plant

Each part of a plant is well suited to the job it does.

This plant is a **buttercup**. Look at its different parts and their **functions** (what they do).

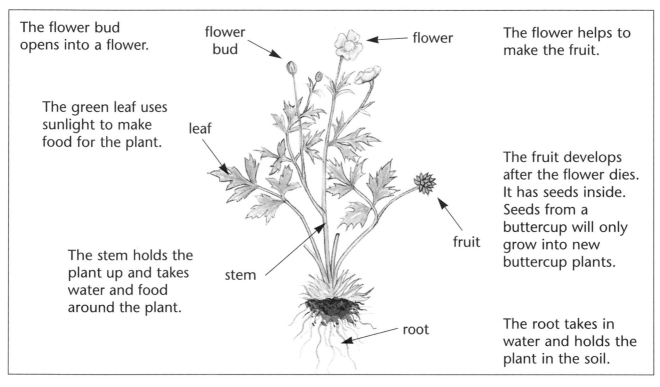

The flower bud opens into a flower.

flower bud

flower

The flower helps to make the fruit.

The green leaf uses sunlight to make food for the plant.

leaf

The fruit develops after the flower dies. It has seeds inside. Seeds from a buttercup will only grow into new buttercup plants.

fruit

The stem holds the plant up and takes water and food around the plant.

stem

The root takes in water and holds the plant in the soil.

root

All flowering plants have **roots**, **stems**, **leaves**, **flowers** and **fruit**. The shapes of each of these change in different plants but they all do the same job.

1 Write down the names of four of the groups of living things we call plants.

2 List three things that all plants do. Begin your sentence 'All plants can …'

3 A daffodil plant grows from a bulb with little roots. Draw and label the bud, flower, fruit, leaf and stem of this plant.

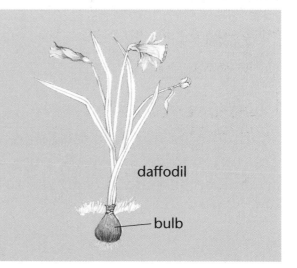

daffodil

bulb

Seed dispersal

Seeds need space to grow into healthy plants. They have to be moved away from the plant where they grew. The seeds can be **scattered** by animals, wind or by **pods** bursting open. All plants make lots of seeds, but only a few seeds grow into healthy plants.

How are seeds scattered?

By animals

All fruits have seeds inside.
Some birds eat brightly coloured fruits.
Some seeds are hard outside so they pass through the birds' guts and are dropped on the ground.

rose hip

elderberry

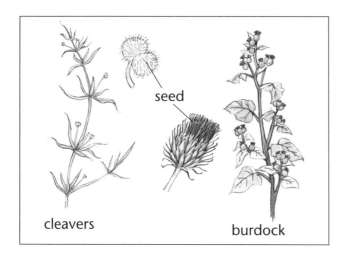

seed

cleavers

burdock

These seeds have little hooks that stick to animals' fur.

Many animals like to eat seeds.

Squirrels bury nuts in a food store. They often forget where the nuts are hidden and the nuts grow into new plants.

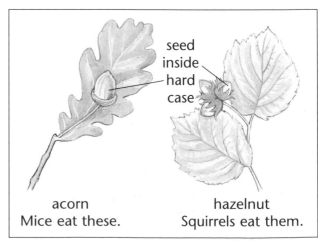

seed inside hard case

acorn
Mice eat these.

hazelnut
Squirrels eat them.

By wind

These seeds are light so they can be blown away.

They are joined to a wing or a **parachute** which helps them to catch the wind.

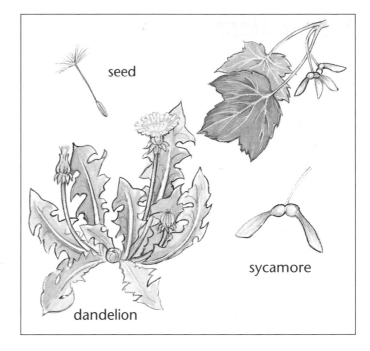

seed

sycamore

dandelion

By explosion

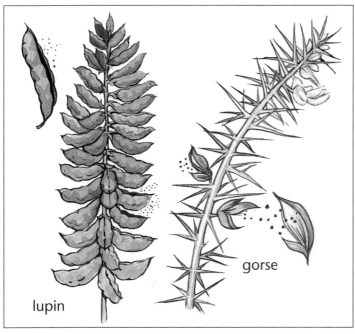

lupin

gorse

These seeds grow in a **pod**. When they are **ripe** the pod dries and bursts open or explodes. This flings the seeds away from the plant they grew on.

1 Explain why seeds need to be moved away from the plant they grew on.

2 How does the shape of dandelion seeds and burdock seeds help them to be moved away from the plant?

3 Why do the seeds inside rose hip fruits need to be hard outside?

Growing plants

Seeds need water and warmth to begin to grow or **germinate**. Seeds will germinate without light, but light is needed for the **seedlings** to grow into healthy plants. All plants need light, water and the right temperature to continue growing.

What do seeds need to grow?

When seeds start to grow they produce tiny roots and shoots. This is called **germination**. Later they produce leaves and grow bigger.

Red class grew some cress seeds. They investigated what the seeds needed to grow into healthy plants. They tested the effect of light, water and temperature.

Seeds without light
Tom's group gave their seeds water and kept them in the warm classroom. They put them in a dark cupboard.

The seeds did germinate but they are tall and pale.

After four days

The seeds did not germinate.

After four days

Seeds without water
Clare's group put their seeds on the light window sill in the warm classroom. They did not water the seeds.

Seeds without warmth
Sara's group watered their seeds but they put them in the refrigerator.

The seeds did not germinate.

After four days

28

Seeds with light, water and warmth

Daniel's group put their seeds in the warm classroom on the light window sill and watered them.

These seeds all germinated and grew well.

After four days

Growing the cress seedlings

Red class wanted to grow their cress plants to make cress sandwiches. Only those **seedlings** that had light, water and warmth grew into healthy plants that they could eat.

light

the right amount of water

warmth

▲ *All plants need these things in order to grow well.*

1 Michelle planted some bean seeds in her garden in December. They did not grow. Why do you think they did not grow? Begin your sentence 'I think Michelle's bean seeds did not grow because ...'

2 Yasmin planted some sunflower seeds in her garden. The seeds in the sunny flower bed grew well. The seeds under the shady tree did not. Explain why.

3 Write down two things seeds need to germinate.

4 Write down three things seedlings need to grow into healthy plants.

Designed to survive

Plants of the same **species** (such as all dandelions) may grow in different places. They may grow to a different size or a different shape because of the conditions there. We say the plants have **adapted** to living in these places.

How a dandelion plant survives

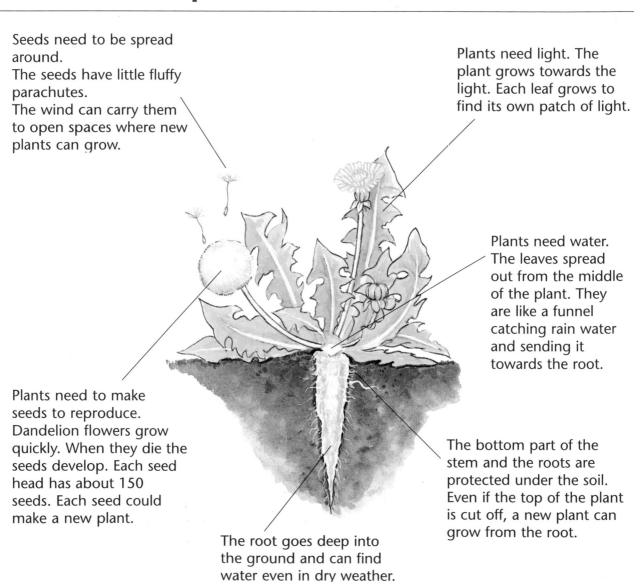

Seeds need to be spread around.
The seeds have little fluffy parachutes.
The wind can carry them to open spaces where new plants can grow.

Plants need light. The plant grows towards the light. Each leaf grows to find its own patch of light.

Plants need water. The leaves spread out from the middle of the plant. They are like a funnel catching rain water and sending it towards the root.

Plants need to make seeds to reproduce. Dandelion flowers grow quickly. When they die the seeds develop. Each seed head has about 150 seeds. Each seed could make a new plant.

The bottom part of the stem and the roots are protected under the soil. Even if the top of the plant is cut off, a new plant can grow from the root.

The root goes deep into the ground and can find water even in dry weather.

Growing in different places

How are dandelion plants different?
Mina and Jack went to look for dandelions.

They found them growing on the field, by the hedge and in the rose bed. They compared the plants and looked for differences. They saw that the dandelions from the different places were **adapted** to where they lived.

◀ *On the **mown** field.*

The plants grew close to the ground where they miss being cut by the **mower**. The leaves spread flat. Some plants had flowers and seeds. The seed heads grew tall.

By the shady hedge. ▶

The plants grew tall to get more light. The leaves were large and thin. The flowers and seed heads were small.

◀*In the sunny rose bed.*

The plants were big because they had lots of light and water. There were few plants to get in their way. They had lots of leaves and flowers and seed heads.

1 Write a sentence saying what new dandelion plants can grow from.

2 Describe what dandelion plants growing in a shady place would look like.

3 Say why you think dandelion plants are much shorter when they grow in fields grazed by sheep.

A place to live

Different animals live in different places. They have to be able to find food and water. Many need air to breathe and they also need a place to hide from other animals that would eat them. Animals are especially adapted to the place where they live.

What do snails like?

Tom and Clare looked for snails in the garden.

They found some hiding in a damp corner among the stones and logs.

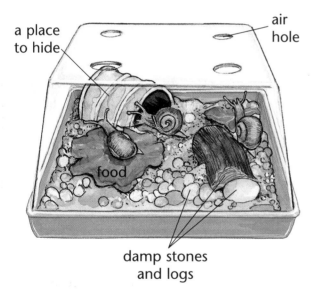

a place to hide

air hole

food

damp stones and logs

▲ A plant **propagator** has space for snails to move around.

They decided to keep some snails in the classroom to study them. The container they chose was a good place for the snails to live. This is called their **environment**.

We cleaned the container out and gave the snails fresh food every day.

We made damp dark places for our snails to hide.

We took the snails back to their garden environment when we had finished studying them.

How are snails adapted?

Snails are well suited to the environment where they live.

Snails have a soft slimy **muscular** body.

They make slime to slide easily over rough stones.

They eat by scraping away the soft parts of plants with their hard dark tongue, called a **radula**.

They have a hard shell and can draw their whole body inside to hide.

In winter they make a tough layer across the bottom of the shell which protects them from the cold.

They use their feelers to touch and explore as they move.

They can protect their feelers and eyes by drawing them into their body.

They breathe by opening and closing their breathing hole.

Snails lay soft white eggs hidden in the soil which hatch out into tiny baby snails.

1 Explain what an environment is. Begin your sentence 'An environment is ...'

2 Write a sentence describing what snails need in their environment.

3 Describe how the snail's body helps it to move over rough stones.

4 Write down three things snails can do to protect themselves.

Living together

Plants and animals live together in different places or **habitats**.
Each habitat has groups of animals and plants that need each other to
survive. Animals use the plants for shelter and food. Some live there
all the time, others just visit the habitat and then go away again.

Look at this hedgerow habitat

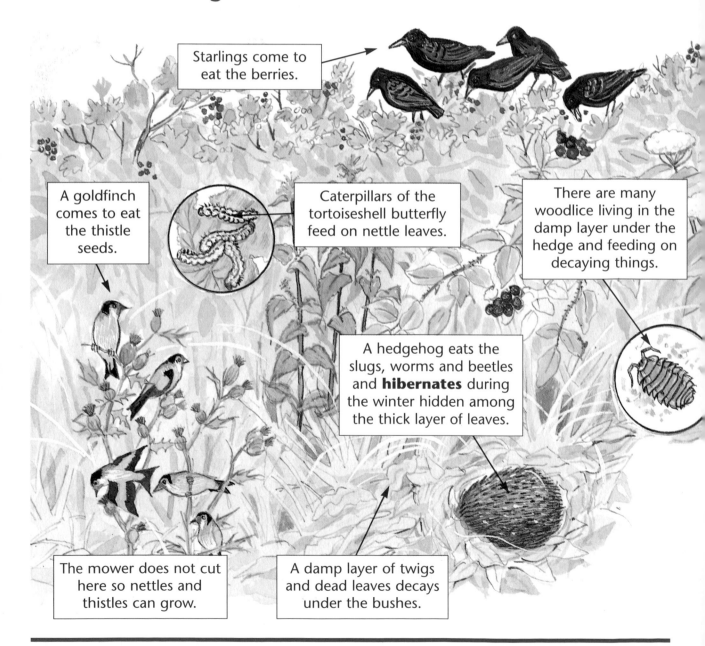

Starlings come to
eat the berries.

A goldfinch
comes to eat
the thistle
seeds.

Caterpillars of the
tortoiseshell butterfly
feed on nettle leaves.

There are many
woodlice living in the
damp layer under the
hedge and feeding on
decaying things.

A hedgehog eats the
slugs, worms and beetles
and **hibernates** during
the winter hidden among
the thick layer of leaves.

The mower does not cut
here so nettles and
thistles can grow.

A damp layer of twigs
and dead leaves decays
under the bushes.

Hawthorn bushes were planted around a field to make a hedge. Look how many different plants are growing there now. No-one planted them! All these plants grew from seeds. There are lots of different plants here so many animals come too. They find food in the hedge and a place to shelter and have their young. Many animals come to feed on the plants but some feed on the animals that come to the hedge.

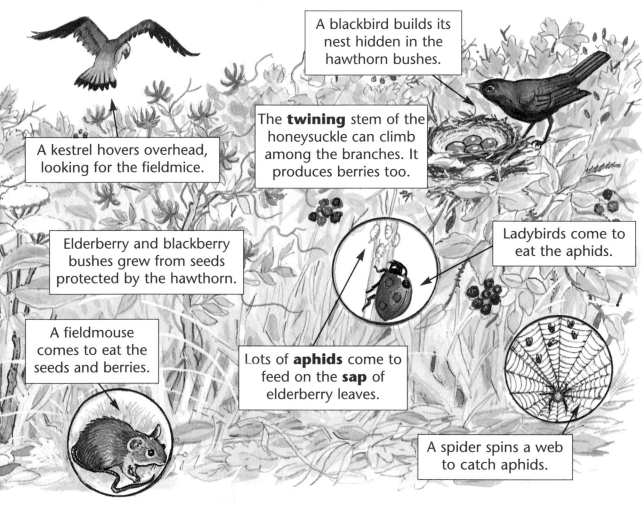

A blackbird builds its nest hidden in the hawthorn bushes.

A kestrel hovers overhead, looking for the fieldmice.

The **twining** stem of the honeysuckle can climb among the branches. It produces berries too.

Elderberry and blackberry bushes grew from seeds protected by the hawthorn.

Ladybirds come to eat the aphids.

A fieldmouse comes to eat the seeds and berries.

Lots of **aphids** come to feed on the **sap** of elderberry leaves.

A spider spins a web to catch aphids.

1 Explain why lots of different plants grow in the hedge.

2 Write down five different animals living in the hedge. Next to each animal write down why it comes there.

3 Write down some animals that eat plants in the hedge. Write down some that eat other animals.

4 Write down what you think would happen to the animals if the hedge was cut down.

Test your knowledge

1 Fill in the shaded boxes to make words that say what all plants do.

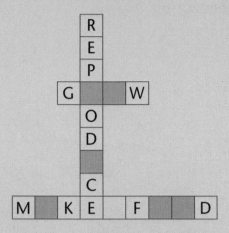

```
        R
        E
        P
    G [ ] [ ] W
        O
        D
        C
M [ ] K E [ ] F [ ] [ ] D
```

2 Copy these sentences then draw arrows to join them correctly. One has been done for you.

The flower   takes in water.

The stem   **helps to make the fruit.**

The root   **uses sunlight to make food.**

The green leaf **has seeds inside.**

The fruit   **holds the plant up.**

3 Mina found this plant in the school cupboard after the holidays. What should she do to make it grow better?

4 Where do I live?

in a hedge	in the pond	under a stone

Write down these sentences and choose one of the boxes above to finish them.

a I have a long streamlined body, I have gills and fins, I have a strong tail for swimming. I live ....

b I have feathery wings, I eat fruit and berries with my strong beak, I need a safe place to build my nest. I live ....

c I eat rotting wood, I have to keep my body damp, I like cool, dark places. I need to hide from birds that would eat me. I live ....

5 Choose one of the boxes below to finish the sentence.

a Lupins have seeds in a pod. They ....

b Wood avens have seeds with little hooks. They ....

c Blackberries have hard seeds in juicy fruits. They ....

d Willowherb seeds have a fluffy parachute. They ....

explode and fling the seeds away	get eaten by birds
get stuck to animals' fur	get blown away by the wind

Materials and their properties

Before you start you should know that:

■ materials can be grouped according to simple properties, such as appearance and texture;

■ there are common materials such as metal, plastic, wood and rock, and some of these are found naturally;

■ many materials have a variety of uses;

■ materials are chosen for tasks according to their properties.

In this unit you will learn:

■ more about the properties of materials;

■ about materials that come from plants, animals and under the ground;

■ that some materials can be manufactured to make new products;

■ where soil comes from and what it is made of;

■ about soil drainage;

■ about mixtures and how to separate them by sieving;

■ how to keep things hot or cold by using thermal insulation;

■ about solids, liquids and gases and their properties.

What things are made from

A **material** is the substance from which things are made. You use lots of materials every day. Materials have different **properties**. They might be soft, hard, **waterproof**, **flexible** or **absorbent**. These different properties mean that the materials can be used to do different things.

Different types of materials

You use many different objects both at home and at school, such as knives and forks, chairs and pencil cases, skipping ropes and balls. These objects can be made from metal, wood, glass, plastic, wool or other **materials**. The materials they are made from depends on what they are used for.

Paper towels can be used to soak up liquids in the kitchen. The paper is **absorbent**. Metal wire can be bent and twisted. It is **flexible**.

table
toy
chair

knife, fork and spoon
scissors
saucepan

painting apron
bucket
lunchbox

These objects are often made from wood. Wood has been used because:
- it is hard;
- it is strong;
- it is easy to shape.

These objects are often made of metal. Metal has been used because:
- it can be sharp;
- it doesn't burn;
- it is hard and strong.

These objects have been made from plastic. Plastic has been used because:
- it is **waterproof**;
- it can be **colourful**;
- it can be **moulded** easily.

What are its properties?

Materials are used for different things because of their **properties**. A window is made from glass because glass can let light into a room. One of the useful properties of glass is that it is **transparent**.

> Wood is hard, strong and can be shaped. It is ideal for making a door.

> Wool is warm and soft. It can be dyed into different colours. It is ideal for making hats, gloves and scarves.

Yasmin collected some objects from home and school. She grouped them using the properties of hard and soft.

She could also have grouped them using the properties of **shiny** and **dull**.

hard

soft

dull

shiny

1 Make a list of ten objects that you use every day.
   Write down next to each object in your list what it is made from.
   For example,
   chair   wood

2 Find two different ways to sort the objects in your list using properties. For example, hard and soft or rough and smooth.

Where materials come from

Natural or **raw materials** come from animals, plants or under the ground. Wood can be used in its natural state to make things like lolly sticks or clothes pegs. Wood can also be changed or **manufactured** to make new products like paper.

Materials from plants

Cotton grows on bushes. When it is ripe it is **harvested** and made into **fabric**.

▲ The cotton **bolls** being harvested.

Rubber comes from the **sap** of the rubber tree. The sap is collected and **processed** into rubber which can be used for tyres and elastic bands.

Paper is made from wood. After the trees have been cut down they are taken to the mill and **manufactured** into paper.

◀ The sap being collected from a rubber tree.

Materials from animals

Silk is made by silk moths when they spin their **cocoon**. Silk is a fine **fibre** or thread which can be **woven** into fabric.

Leather, **suede**, wool and fur come from the skins of animals. The skins are processed and turned into clothing.

▲ *The cocoon of the silk moth.*

▲ *Some of the animals from which leather, suede and wool come.*

Materials from under the ground

Iron ore is a **mineral** that is found in rocks under the ground. It is mined and manufactured into metal products such as nails, screws and garden tools.

Slate, flint, **clay** and coal are other materials that come from the ground.

▲ *Iron ore being mined.*

1 Write a list of five materials that come from plants.

2 Draw a shoe and label the raw materials used to make it.

3 Write a list of five objects that can be manufactured from wood.

Soil

Soil is made when rocks are worn down. It is made of **particles** of different sizes. **Clay** particles are very fine and get sticky when they are wet. **Chalk** particles are also fine but do not become sticky when wet. **Sand** particles are bigger and gritty.

Looking at soil

Jack got some **soil** from his garden. He used a hand lens to look at it closely. He saw that the **particles** were different sizes, shapes and colours. He put the soil in a bottle with some water and shook it. At first it was cloudy. The next day he could see different layers.

▲ *Soil and water shaken together.*

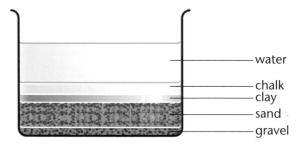

▲ *Soil and water once they have settled.*

Jack went to stay with his grandfather. He wanted to see if the soil there was the same as in his own garden. Jack found that the thickness of each layer was different from his soil. His grandfather's soil had a thinner layer of **sand** and more **clay** and **chalk** than Jack's soil.

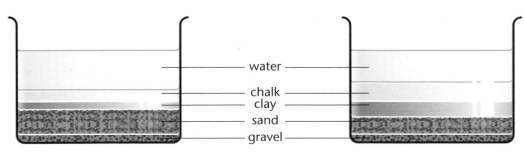

▲ *Jack's soil sample.*   ▲ *Grandfather's soil sample.*

Soil drainage

Jack tested the two soils to see which would let water run through the fastest. His grandfather said that this was testing soil **drainage**. Jack put the same amount of each soil into different funnels and poured 100 ml of water into each one.

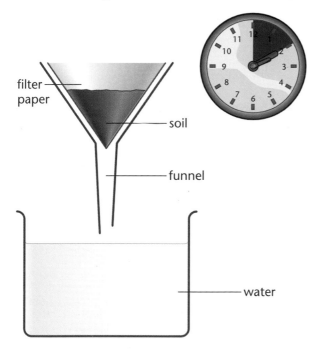

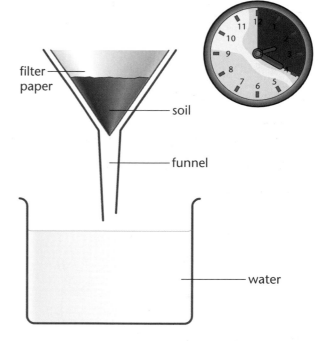

▲ Jack's garden soil let the water through quickly.

▲ His grandfather's soil let the water through much more slowly.

Jack's soil had less clay and more sand than his grandfather's. Sand particles are bigger and have more air spaces between them. The air spaces let the water drain through more quickly.

Grandfather's soil had a lot of clay which is made from very fine particles. The water could only drain through it slowly as there were smaller air spaces between the particles.

1 What is soil?

2 Why do sandy soils let water run through more quickly than clay soils?

3 Jack's teacher gave the class some seeds to take home to grow. On the packet it said that the seeds needed well-drained soil. In whose garden would they grow best, Jack's or his grandfather's? Explain why.

Separating solids

A **mixture** is made when two or more substances are mixed together. Substances in a mixture can be separated. **Sieving** is a way of separating a mixture of two or more dry substances which have particles of different sizes.

Sieves

Sieves are often used in the home. For instance, sieves can be used to separate the lumps from the flour when making cakes. They can also be used in the garden to separate stones from soil to make it easier for seeds to grow.

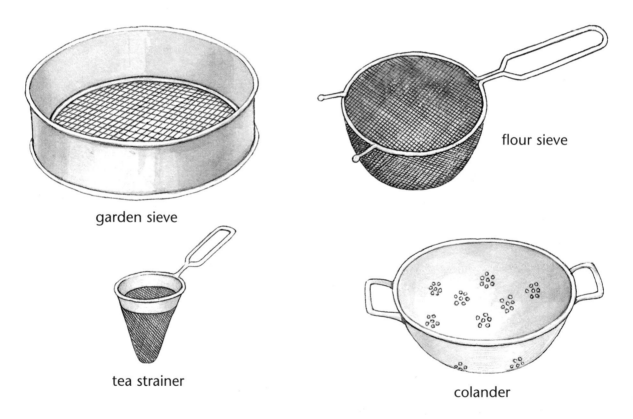

garden sieve

flour sieve

tea strainer

colander

▲ *Sieves have holes of different sizes to suit their purpose.*

If a sieve has large holes it will stop large particles but anything smaller will fall through.

If a sieve has tiny holes it will let only very small particles fall through. Bigger lumps will be trapped in the sieve.

Separating a mixture of solids

Sara's teacher noticed that the jars of rice, sand and stones that the class used for science had tipped over. She gave Sara the **mixture** and asked her to separate the three substances. As the mixture was made up of dry particles, Sara chose two different sieves to help her with the task.

She chose to use a sieve with large holes first. This let through the rice and sand but trapped the stones.

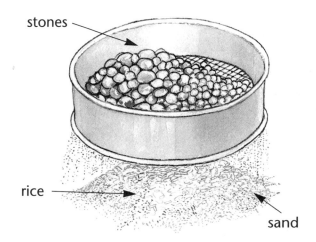

stones

rice

sand

Her second choice was a sieve with medium-sized holes. This one trapped the rice but let the fine particles of sand pass through.

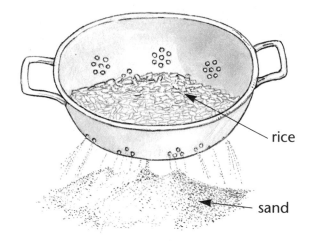

rice

sand

Using the process of **sieving**, Sara successfully separated the mixture of dry substances for her teacher.

1 What is a mixture?

2 What is the purpose of a sieve?

3 If you had a mixture of sugar, rice and pasta bows, how would you separate the three substances?

Keeping things hot or cold

Materials which are used to keep things hot or cold are called **thermal insulators**. Heat cannot easily pass through layers of thermal **insulation**. A hot substance which is **insulated** will stay hot. A cold substance which is insulated stays cold because the insulation keeps the heat out.

Keeping things hot

Some materials are good for keeping the heat in. We use fabrics like these for our winter clothing.

These materials are called **thermal insulators** because they do not let the heat pass through easily. We also say they are poor **conductors** of heat. They trap the heat around the object that they are keeping warm.

woolly scarf

woolly hat

fur-lined gloves

padded snowsuit

leather boots

Sometimes layers of material are used to keep things warm. These layers work well because air is trapped between each layer. Air is a poor conductor of heat and so the layers **insulate** the object.

outer waterproof layer

air spaces which are poor heat conductors

layer of **polyester** and **viscose** padding

inner cotton lining

▲ *The layers and air spaces in a ski jacket which is a good thermal insulator.*

Keeping things cold

Thermal insulators are also good for keeping things cold. This is useful when we want to stop frozen things from **melting**. If we leave them in a warm place, they will get hotter.

An ice lolly **wrapped** in a thick layer of a thermal insulator (or lots of thin layers) will stay frozen for quite a long time because the **insulation** keeps the heat around it out.

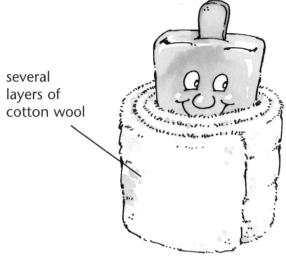

several layers of cotton wool

An ice lolly which is not wrapped in a thermal insulator will quickly melt because the heat around it can get in.

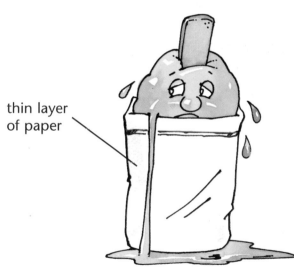

thin layer of paper

Remember that heat travels. Thermal insulators stop this happening by stopping the heat **escaping** or **entering**.

1 Why are fish and chips wrapped in layers of paper?

2 Why are layers of thermal insulation better than one layer?

3 Why does a wrapped ice lolly stay cold longer than one which is not wrapped?

Solids, liquids and gases

All materials are either a **solid**, a **liquid** or a **gas**.
Solids keep their shape unless a **force** is **applied** to them.
Liquids pour and take the shape of the container they are in.
Gases spread out and fill all the space around them.

Solids

Solids are made of particles which are packed together very tightly.

Daniel had four balls of **plasticine**, all of the same shape, size and weight. As plasticine is a solid, he could change the shape of the balls only by applying a **force**. He used pushes and pulls. Although he changed the shape, the amount of plasticine was still the same.

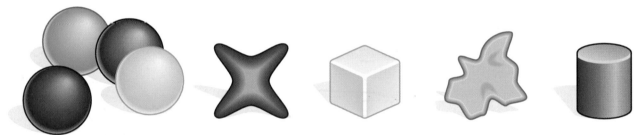

Liquids

Liquids are made of particles that are not packed as tightly as those in a solid. So a liquid can pour and take up a different shape. Mina had 100 ml of water. She poured it into a tall, thin container. The water took the shape of the container. Then she poured it into other containers. Each time the water took the shape of the container.

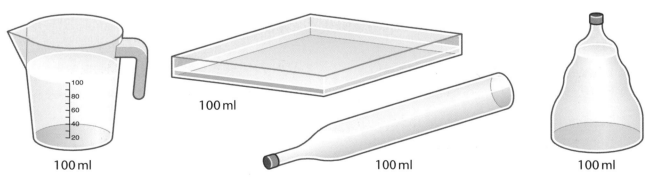

100 ml

100 ml

100 ml

100 ml

Gases

Gases cannot usually be seen. To prove they are there Daniel put an empty bottle into a bowl of water. He noticed that bubbles were coming out of the bottle. These were air bubbles. The bottle was not empty, it was full of air.

Gases have particles which are loosely joined together. They spread out to fill all the space available.

Mina sprayed some **perfume** into the corner of a room. She asked Daniel to stand in another corner and tell her when he could smell the perfume. Mina could smell it straight away. As the perfume slowly spread across the room Daniel could smell it too.

1 Name two solids, two liquids and two gases you use every day.

2 Explain in your own words why solids, liquids and gases behave differently.

3 Why couldn't Daniel smell the perfume at the same time as Mina?

Test your knowledge

1 Think about a room that you know well.

Imagine that the furniture is made from materials with unsuitable properties. For example, the legs of a chair could be made from a soft and flexible material like sponge!

Draw each piece of furniture and label the material and its properties.

2 Sort the following materials into three groups.

The first group is **materials which come from animals**.

The second group is **materials which come from plants**.

The third group is **materials which come from under the ground**.

Make three lists, one for each group.

slate	**wool**	**coal**	**gold**
silk	**cotton**	**linen**	**corn oil**
clay	**olive oil**	**pearl**	**diamond**
fur	**leather**	**ivory**	**rubber**

3 Collect some soil from different places. Use a hand lens to look carefully at the particles. Notice their colour, size and shape. Draw exactly what you can see.

4 Grow seeds in different kinds of soil. You could use sand, chalk or clay soils. Compare your plants every week, draw each plant and measure it.

Which seeds grew best? Explain in your own words why these seeds grew best.

5 Grow seeds in sieved soil and in lumpy soil.

Do seeds grown in sieved soil grow better than those in lumpy soil? Explain in your own words why this happened.

6 Design a container that will stop ice lollies melting on a picnic.

Draw your container and label the materials you would use. Explain how your container would work.

7 Find out how long the smell of perfume takes to travel across a small room.

Try this again in a larger area like your school hall. What did you find out?

What happens if you spray perfume in the open air?

Changes in materials

Before you start you should know that:

■ objects made from some materials can be changed in shape by squashing, bending, twisting and stretching;

■ everyday materials such as bread and clay can be changed when they are heated or cooled.

In this unit you will learn:

■ that mixing materials can make reversible or irreversible changes;

■ about dissolving and soluble substances such as salt and sugar;

■ what a saturated solution is;

■ how to make sugar dissolve more quickly;

■ about filtering as a way of separating insoluble substances from liquids;

■ how to make different types of filter;

■ about evaporation and how to speed up this process;

■ that evaporation can be used to get soluble substances back from a solution;

■ about thermometers and their uses;

■ that melting is the change in state from solid to liquid;

■ that freezing is the change in state from liquid to solid.

Mixing materials

Mixing materials can make them change. Some changes are **reversible**. This means that you can get back the materials you started with. Some changes are **irreversible**. This means that you cannot get back the materials that you started with.

Looking at powders

Tom collected some **powders** – flour, cocoa, salt, sand and **plaster of Paris**. He looked at each powder with a hand lens. He saw that they were different colours and that the **grains** were of different sizes. The flour was very **fine** and the sand was **coarse**.

Tom wanted to see what would happen to each of his powders if he mixed them with water. He stirred half a teaspoon of each powder into different containers of water. He saw that some materials disappeared, or sank, or floated and some changed the colour of the water.

flour   cocoa   salt   sand   plaster of Paris

Irreversible changes

Tom saw that the plaster of Paris had sunk to the bottom of the container and had become solid. His teacher said that the powder had been **chemically changed** and could not be turned back to powder. The change was **irreversible**.

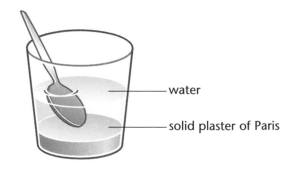

water

solid plaster of Paris

Reversible changes

Tom looked at the sand and water mixture with his hand lens. The grains had settled at the bottom of the container. His teacher said that he could separate the sand and water by **filtering**.

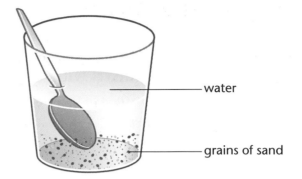

water

grains of sand

Tom looked at the salt water solution. He could not see the salt grains – they had **dissolved**. Tom left some of the mixture in a warm place. A week later the water had gone but the salt grains were back!

The change was **reversible**.

salty water

The flour and the cocoa powder changed the colour of the water. They had formed a **suspension**. The next day the flour grains and the cocoa grains had settled at the bottom of their containers. They had not dissolved.

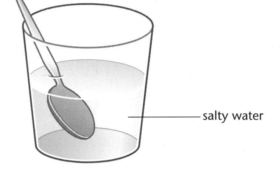

flour held in suspension

cocoa held in suspension

1 Why couldn't Tom get his powdered plaster of Paris back?

2 Which of his materials would he be able to get back in their powdered form?

3 Which of these form a suspension and which make a solution – sand, flour, salt, cocoa and plaster of Paris?

Dissolving

Dissolving is what happens when solids spread out to become part of the liquid they are mixed with. Solids that dissolve in a liquid are called **soluble** substances. Salt is a soluble substance because it dissolves in water.

Mixing sugar with water

Tom remembered what happened when he mixed salt with water. After a little stirring he could no longer see the salt. It had **dissolved** and become part of the liquid. He decided to test other powders to see if they dissolve. Solids that dissolve in a liquid are called **soluble** substances.

I will try to dissolve **granulated** sugar. My father always stirs a spoonful of this into his tea or coffee to make it sweet.

When Tom looked in the cupboard he found the granulated sugar as well as some other sugars. There was icing sugar, brown sugar and lump sugar. He tested each one to see if it would dissolve in water.

Tom stirred half a teaspoon of each of his sugars into 100 ml of water to make a solution. He watched them closely and saw that all of them dissolved. He found that sugar is a **soluble** substance. **Solubility** is one of the properties of sugar.

What makes sugar dissolve faster?

Tom tried adding more sugar to his mixture. After he had added a lot of sugar he found that however hard he stirred, no more sugar would dissolve. His teacher explained that if too much sugar is added to the liquid, only some of it will dissolve. When no more solid will dissolve the solution is **saturated**.

I have added some more water to the saturated solution. Now more sugar can dissolve because there is enough water.

Tom added sugar to cold, warm and hot water. He noticed that the sugar in the hot water dissolved more quickly than the sugar in the warm or cold water. The sugar in the cold water took the longest to dissolve.

cold water

warm water

hot water

300
250
200
150
100
50

jug

stop watch

sugar

1 Name two solids that are soluble.

2 What is a saturated solution?

3 Can you think of three ways to make sugar dissolve faster? Write down how you would make this happen. Draw pictures and label what is happening in each case.

Filtering

Solids that do not dissolve in a liquid are **insoluble** substances. These may sink to the bottom or stay in suspension in the water. Insoluble substances can be separated from liquids by **filtering**.

Making a filter

Tom wanted to find out whether he could separate his mixture of sand and water.

Sand is an **insoluble** substance because it does not dissolve in water. The grains had settled at the bottom of the container.

▲ *Mixture of sand and water.*

Tom used some **filter paper** and a funnel to **filter** his mixture. Filter paper has very small holes which let tiny particles through but trap larger particles. Tom cut out a circle from the filter paper. He folded the circle in half, and then in half again to make a **cone**.

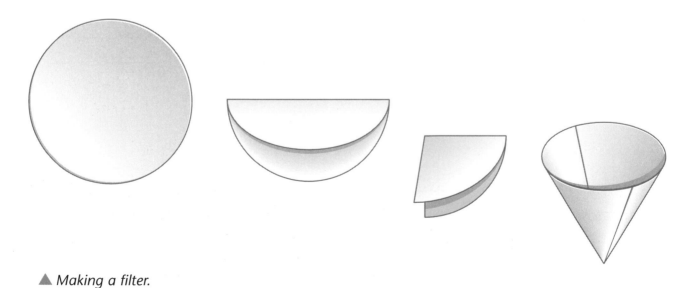

▲ *Making a filter.*

Using a filter

Tom opened the cone so that it fitted inside the funnel. He put the funnel over a container. Then he carefully poured the sand mixture into the filter paper cone. Tom watched as the water dripped through the tiny holes in the filter paper into the container.

▲ *Filtering the sand from the water.*

Tom's mixture had been **separated** by the filter. The water went through the paper into the container and the sand was trapped in the filter paper. Tom carefully removed the filter paper which held the sand and left it to dry.

Tom used up all the filter paper so he looked for other materials to use as filters. He tried cotton wool, gravel and sand. He found that these materials could also separate his insoluble substances by trapping the particles.

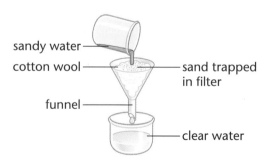

▲ *Cotton wool filter.*

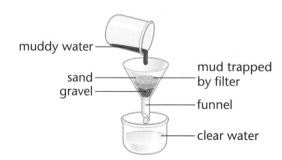

▲ *Sand and gravel filter.*

1 What did Tom's mixture contain at the start?

2 What was trapped in the filter paper?

3 What passed through the filter paper?

4 Do you think the other materials Tom used as filters were better or worse than the filter paper? Explain why you think this.

Evaporating

Soluble substances like salt and sugar can be separated from liquids by the process of **evaporation**. As the water in the solution gets warm, tiny droplets of it turn into a gas called **water vapour**. The water vapour becomes part of the air leaving the salt or sugar behind.

Puddles

Tom saw that rain made **puddles** on his school playground. When the rain stopped, the puddles got smaller and dried up. Tom used chalk to draw round a puddle every hour to see what happened.

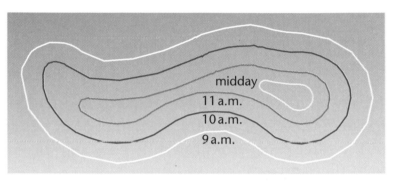

midday
11 a.m.
10 a.m.
9 a.m.

▲ Tom's puddle became smaller.

Tom's teacher said that the puddle dried up because the water **evaporated**. It turned into a gas and went into the air. The gas is called **water vapour**.

Evaporation causes washing to dry when it is hung out on the line on a sunny or windy day. On a hot day the water evaporates more quickly.

Evaporation can be speeded up.

On a hot day the **higher temperature** makes the water evaporate more quickly.	26 °C
A **breeze** blows the vapour away from the puddle so that more water vapour can move into the air.	3 ▶

Can we get the sugar back?

Tom wondered if he could use evaporation to separate his sugar and water solution. He poured some of his sugar solution into a shallow dish. Tom put the dish next to the window where he knew it would be sunny and warm.

▲ 9:30 a.m.   ▲ 3:30 p.m.   ▲ next morning

Tom found that the water did evaporate. It dried up and left a layer of sugar in the dish. Tom carefully scraped the powdery sugar from the dish. The sugar was left behind because only the water could evaporate.

Tom tried the same test with some salt water. He weighed 5 g of salt and made a solution with water. He left it to evaporate and found that 5 g of salt was left after the water had gone.

Tom remembered that when he had paddled in the sea in his canvas shoes, the shoes had dried with a white mark on them. This was salt left on the shoes after the salty sea water had evaporated.

1 Write in your own words what happened to the water from Tom's puddle.

2 How can you speed up the process of evaporation? Draw and label pictures of two ways.

3 What is the best weather for washing to be hung outside to dry? Explain why in your own words.

Thermometers

Thermometers can be used to measure the temperature of solids, liquids or gases. The liquid in the thermometer rises as it gets warmer. The number of **degrees Celsius** (°C) will be higher as it gets warmer and lower as it gets colder.

Looking at a thermometer

If you look closely at a **thermometer** you will see a thin line of coloured liquid inside. The numbers beside the liquid are the **scale** measured in **degrees Celsius**. We write this °C.

If you hold the **bulb** end of the thermometer in your hand, the level of the liquid rises. This is because the heat from your hand warms the liquid and makes it rise.

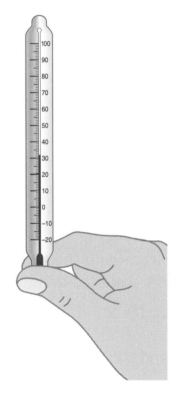

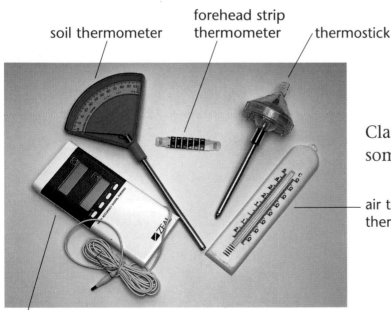

soil thermometer

forehead strip thermometer

thermostick

Clare's teacher showed the class some thermometers.

air temperature thermometer

digital thermometer

Using a thermometer to record temperature

Clare used a thermometer to measure the temperature of the air in different parts of her school. She made sure that she waited for the liquid inside the thermometer to stop rising or falling before she wrote down the temperatures. She put the results in a table.

Part of school	Temperature
Clare's classroom	22 °C
cloakroom	20 °C
stock cupboard	19 °C
near the radiator	30 °C
in the fridge	4 °C
playground	8 °C

When Clare had **chicken pox** her mum kept a chart of Clare's temperature each day.

Clare started to feel ill on Tuesday when her temperature began to rise.

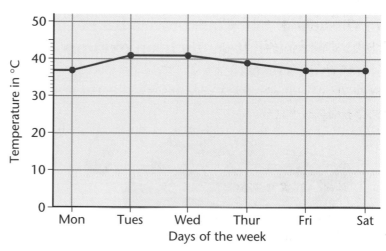

▲ Line graph.

1 Explain in your own words how a thermometer works.

2 Draw a bar chart to show the temperatures in the different parts of Clare's school. Which part was warmest? Which part was coldest?

3 Why were each of the temperatures in Clare's school different?

4 Look at the line graph of Clare's daily temperatures and answer these questions.

  a What is Clare's normal body temperature?

  b What was Clare's highest temperature when she was ill?

  c How long was Clare's temperature above normal?

Melting and freezing

Melting and **freezing** are reversible processes. When a material melts it **changes state** from a solid to a liquid – ice melts to become water. When a material freezes it changes state from a liquid to a solid – water freezes to become ice.

Melting

When a solid is heated it **changes state** and becomes a liquid. This process is called **melting**. When the heat is removed, the liquid cools down and becomes solid again. For example, wax melts when it is hot and becomes solid again when it cools.

The children in Clare's class were making some chocolate shapes for the school fair. Clare broke a bar of chocolate into pieces. Then she melted it gently in an **ovenproof** dish that she put in a pan of hot water.

Clare poured the melted chocolate into a **mould** and left it to cool. The chocolate became solid again but had a new shape!

She knew that although the shape had changed, the amount of chocolate was the same.

Freezing

Freezing makes a liquid change state into a solid. Water freezes at a temperature of **zero** degrees Celsius (0 °C). Other liquids freeze at different temperatures.

The children in Clare's class were also making iced drinks to sell at the fair. They wanted to make different shapes and **flavours** of ice. They used orange juice, lemon squash, milk and cola. They poured the liquids into fruit-shaped moulds and left them in the freezer overnight.

Clare wondered if she could make a material freeze without putting it somewhere very cold. Her teacher lit a candle and they watched the wax carefully.

As the wax was heated it melted and became a liquid that ran down the candle. As the wax cooled it became a solid again. This showed Clare that wax freezes as it cools, without being in a very cold place.

1 Write down two processes that are reversible.

2 Why does wax set on the side of a candle? Draw pictures and label them to show what happens.

3 Describe how you can make a solid melt.

4 Look at the Glossary to help you explain what the words in bold mean.

Test your knowledge

1 Make a collection of powders, for example baking powder, bicarbonate of soda, talcum powder, coffee and washing powder. Write down the name of each powder in a list. Next to each powder in your list write down what happens when it is added to water.

2 Can you get any of your powders back from the water? Write down how you could do this for each of your powders.

Clue – you could use filtering with different filters or evaporation.

Now try your ideas and record your results.

3 Find out how much salt you can add to 50 ml of water before it becomes a saturated solution. Measure 50 ml of water. Add a teaspoon of salt and stir until it has all dissolved. Keep doing this until no more salt will dissolve. How many teaspoons of salt did you use?

4 Pour 250 ml of water into a shallow dish. Pour another 250 ml of water into a deep container. Put them in the same warm place. Which one evaporates fastest? Try to explain your results.

5 Use the library to help you find answers to these questions.

a What is the melting temperature of iron ore?

b Why does molten lava freeze as it moves further from a volcano?

c Why doesn't a penguin's blood freeze in the cold climate where it lives?

d Why is salt spread on icy roads in winter?

Try to find more fascinating facts about melting and freezing.

6 Read the temperature on each of the four thermometers below. Match each temperature to the place where the temperature was recorded.

a freezer
on a radiator
a cup of tea
a healthy human

All about forces

Before you start you should know that:

■ pushes and pulls make things move;

■ a push will make an object move away from you;

■ a pull will make an object move towards you;

■ pushes and pulls are examples of forces;

■ forces can make moving objects speed up, slow down or stop;

■ forces can make moving objects move in a different direction;

■ forces can change the shape of objects.

In this unit you will learn:

■ that twists and turns are examples of forces;

■ that weight is a force caused by gravity acting upon the mass of an object;

■ that air resistance is a force that opposes gravity;

■ that when springs and elastic bands are stretched they exert a force on whatever is stretching them;

■ that when springs are squashed they exert a force on whatever is squashing them;

■ that forces have both size and direction;

■ that when forces acting on a stationary object balance, the object will not move;

■ that when forces acting on a stationary object are unbalanced, the object will start to move;

■ about how forces can make an object float or sink;

■ how magnets can attract and repel each other;

■ that magnets attract magnetic materials.

What can forces do?

Pushes, **pulls**, **turns** and **twists** are all examples of **forces**. When one or more of these act on an object they can make it move, stop it moving, change its shape or its **speed**. If you look carefully all around you now, you will see forces in action.

What happens when you push or pull an object?

Some objects are **stationary** – they are not moving. If you give a push or a pull to a stationary object you might make it:

■ start to move;
■ change its shape.

If you push or pull a moving object you might make it:

■ stop moving or slow down;
■ move quicker;
■ change direction;
■ change its shape even more.

What is the difference between a turn and a twist?

Forces can also be used to **turn** and **twist** an object.

One push or pull can make an object turn around. It stays in the same spot but each part now faces in a new direction. This happens when you balance a ruler on a table.

When an object is twisted, its top end turns one way and its bottom end turns the other way. Two turns are needed to make an object twist.

Where can you see the effects of forces?

You cannot actually see a force, but you can see what it can do. Forces change the **speed**, direction or shape of objects.

Look at the children playing in the school playground. Look for the pushes and pulls, twists and turns. Which objects are starting to move, speeding up, slowing down, changing direction, twisting, turning or becoming a different shape?

1 Write down seven sentences which explain all the things which might happen when a force acts on an object. An example is 'When my dad pushed his car, it started to move.'

2 Explain the difference between a turn and a twist. You can draw pictures to help you explain this.

3 Look at the playground picture again. Write down a list of all of the things forces are causing to happen. Sort them into a table which shows the pushes, pulls, turns and twists. One has been done for you.

Pushes	Pulls	Turns	Twists
		turning skipping rope	

Gravity

Gravity is a force that pulls all objects towards the centre of the Earth. Objects with a greater **mass** are pulled towards the Earth with a greater force. The force **exerted** on an object by gravity is called its **weight**. **Air resistance** is a force that acts in the opposite direction to gravity.

Can you feel the force?

If you balance a heavy book on your hand you can feel the **weight** of the book pushing down. The weight of the book is a force caused by **gravity**. You have to push up on the book with an equal force to stop it from falling to the ground.

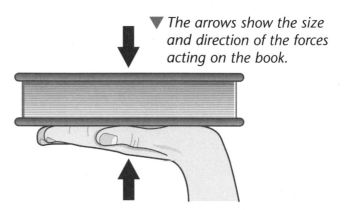

▼ *The arrows show the size and direction of the forces acting on the book.*

Why do some objects weigh more than others?

Feel the force of these objects pushing down on your hand.

Light object ⟶ *Heavy object*

▲ *Gravity pulls harder on heavier objects.*

Heavy objects push down with a greater force than light objects because they have a greater **mass**. Mass is measured in grams. Gravity **exerts** a greater force on objects with a greater mass. This force on an object, caused by gravity, is called its **weight**. The bag of sugar will weigh more than the butter because the bag of sugar has a greater mass.

Which forces act on falling objects?

Objects fall because the force of gravity pulls them towards the Earth. Some objects fall straight down but others spin or twist or drift down to Earth, moving in a zig-zag pattern. Air pushes up against a falling object making the object slow down. This force is called **air resistance**.

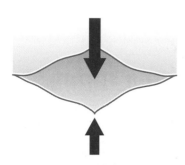

▲ *A piece of paper drifts down, moving in a zig-zag. There is a lot of air pushing up underneath it.*

▲ *A ball of paper falls straight down because less air can push up underneath it.*

The way things fall depends on their shape and size.

About 400 years ago a famous scientist called **Galileo** dropped some objects from the **Leaning Tower of Pisa**. He found out that objects of the same shape take the same time to fall to the ground, even if one is heavy and one is light. The air resistance is the same.

1 Imagine you are holding a block of **polystyrene** on one hand and a brick on the other. Which is harder to hold up? Write down in your own words why one is harder to hold up.

2 What did the scientist Galileo find out about falling objects?

3 Which of these objects will have greater air resistance if you drop them?
- A frisbee or a tennis ball?
- A folded tablecloth or an open tablecloth?

Springs and elastic bands

Forces can be used to change the shape of a spring by **stretching** or **squashing**. When a force acts on a spring, the spring exerts an equal force in the **opposite** direction. Elastic bands can be used to **compare** the pull of gravity on different objects.

What happens when you pull or push on a spring?

Jack used forces to change the shape of a spring.

▲ *Jack pulled the spring to stretch it.*   ▲ *Jack pushed the spring to squash it.*

When Jack pushed the spring, he felt the spring pushing back against his hands. As he **stretched** the spring, he could feel it pulling back. When Jack let go, the spring returned to its original shape.

What happens when you use a stronger spring?

A stronger spring is harder to **stretch** or **squash**. Jack had to use a greater force to change the shape of this spring. He could feel the force exerted by the spring as it tried to return to its original shape.

How can gravity affect the stretch of an elastic band?

If you hang an object on the end of an elastic band, gravity pulls down on the object and stretches the elastic band. A heavy object will stretch the elastic band more than a light object.

Sara used an elastic band to **compare** the pull of gravity on different things.

- First, she attached an empty pot to an elastic band and measured the length of the band with a rule.
- Then she filled the pot with different objects. She measured the length of the band again to see how much it had stretched.
- She recorded all her measurements in a table.

Here are Sara's results.
What did she find out?

Object pulled by gravity	Length of elastic band
empty pot	8 cm
pot of chalk	18 cm
pot of soil	30 cm
pot of stones	25 cm
pot of conkers	17 cm
pot of sand	34 cm

1 Which forces are acting when you stretch a spring? Draw a picture with arrows to show the forces and write down what is happening.

2 Write down a list of six everyday things that work with a spring.

3 Which of Sara's pots stretched the elastic band the most? Write down in your own words what Sara's results tell you about the force of gravity.

Balanced and unbalanced forces

Every force has a **size** and a **direction**. More than one force at a time can act upon an object. When an object is stationary, the size and direction of the forces acting upon it are **balanced**. When these forces are **unbalanced** the object will move.

Are all forces the same size?

Forces can **vary** in size. Some are big and some are small. The size of a force acting on an object affects how far and how fast the object will move.

▲ Sanjay uses a small force on a stationary ball. It moves in the direction that he kicks it.

▲ Sanjay uses a bigger force on a stationary ball. It goes further and faster in the same direction.

Do all forces act in the same direction?

The direction of a force affects which way an object will move.

▲ Sanjay uses a force on the ball to make it move towards the goal.

▲ Laura uses a force in the opposite direction to make the ball move away from the goal.

The size and direction of a force control the movement of an object.

What happens when forces are balanced?

If two forces of the same size act upon an object in opposite directions, the object will not move. The forces are **balanced**, so they **cancel** each other out.

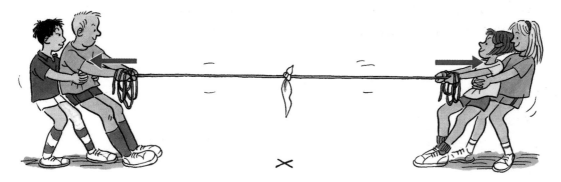

▲ *The two teams pull with equal force in opposite directions. The flag does not move. The two forces are balanced so neither team is winning.*

What happens when forces are unbalanced?

If two forces of different sizes act upon an object in opposite directions, the forces are **unbalanced**. The object will move in the direction of the greater force.

▲ *The two teams pull in opposite directions. The girls' team pulls harder so the forces are unbalanced. The flag moves towards the girls.*

1 Draw two people playing tennis. Write about the size and direction of the forces they apply to the ball. What will happen if one player uses a greater force on the ball?

2 Two boys are arm **wrestling**. Neither is winning. Describe the size and direction of the forces. Are they balanced?

Floating and sinking

When an object **floats** in water, the forces acting upon it are balanced. Gravity pulls downwards on the object and the water pushes upwards with equal force. An object will **sink** if the force of gravity is greater than the **upthrust** of water.

Why do some objects float in water?

Mina put a **polystyrene** block in a tank of water. The block **floated**. When she pushed the block down under the water, she could feel the water pushing the block upwards. This upwards force of water is called **upthrust**.

The block pushes down on the water because gravity is acting on the block. The upthrust of the water pushes up against the block with an equal force. The forces are balanced so the block **floats**.

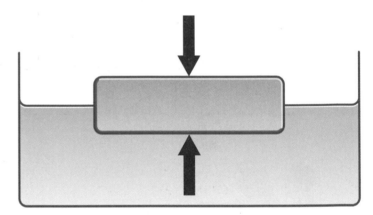

Why do some objects sink in water?

When Mina put a brick in a tank of water the brick **sank**.

The brick is heavy. It has a big mass so the force of gravity acting on it is big. The upthrust of the water is less than the force of gravity. The forces are unbalanced so the brick **sinks**.

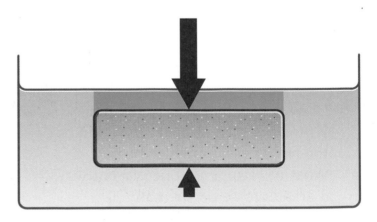

How can you make a sinking object float?

Mina put a ball of **plasticine** into the tank of water. The ball sank. Then she made a boat shape with the plasticine. The boat floated on the water.

The plasticine still has the same mass but the boat shape is bigger because it contains some air. There is more water underneath the boat than underneath the ball. There is more water to push up against the boat.

The upthrust of the water is equal to the downward force of gravity so the boat floats.

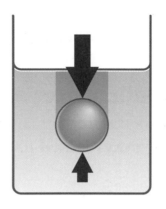

How can you make a floating object sink?

A foil tray will float in a tank of water. If the tray is loaded with stones it will sink.

The stones replace the air in the tray. The stones weigh more than the air so the downward force of gravity is greater.

The upthrust of the water is less than the downward force of gravity so the tray sinks. The forces are unbalanced.

The shape, size and mass of an object affect whether it will float or sink.

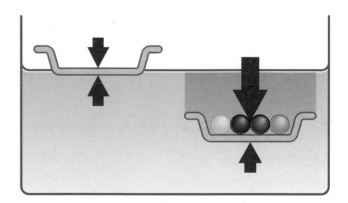

1 A **raft** floats on the water. Draw the raft with arrows to show the forces acting on it. Are the forces balanced?

2 Six people get on the raft and it sinks. Explain why in your own words. Are the forces acting on the raft balanced?

3 A lump of metal is heavy and will sink. Explain in your own words how a heavy metal ship can float.

Magnetic forces

Magnets attract metal materials that contain **iron**. **Cobalt** and **nickel** are also attracted by magnets. All magnets have a North and a South **pole**. The **poles** exert the **magnetic** force. **Opposite** poles **attract** each other, **similar** poles **repel**.

What are magnetic materials?

Magnetic materials are those which are **attracted** by **magnets**. These materials can be **magnetised** to make a magnet.

Magnets attract metal materials, don't they?

Yes, but not *all* metals.
They attract metals which contain **iron**. **Cobalt** and **nickel** are also magnetic materials.

Do all magnets have North and South poles?

Magnets come in different shapes and sizes. The two ends of the magnet exert a strong magnetic force. These are called the **magnetic poles**. All magnets have two poles – a North pole and a South pole.

What forces do magnets exert on each other?

The magnetic poles of magnets can **attract** or **repel** each other. The poles of a magnet are not usually marked 'North' and 'South'. Sometimes they are painted different colours or the North pole is marked with a small dent.

Tom held two magnets like this with **opposite** poles close together. He could feel the magnets pulling towards each other. Opposite poles of magnets attract each other.

If Tom turned one magnet round so that **similar** poles were close together, he would feel the magnets pushing away from each other. Similar poles of magnets repel each other.

How can this magnet float in mid-air?

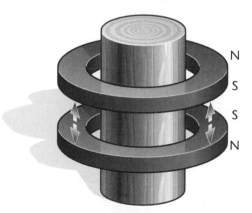

The poles of these magnets are on the flat sides. Similar poles are next to each other on the stick so the magnets repel each other.

1 Which parts of a bar magnet will pick up the most paper clips? What are these parts called?

2 Explain how you would make two magnets attract each other.

3 How could you use magnets to move a toy car without touching it? Draw a picture and write an explanation of how you would do it.

Test your knowledge

1 Matthew threw a ball up into the air. It fell back down to the ground. Draw a picture and write about the forces involved.

2 Draw two boats, one floating on the water and one starting to sink. Show what is making the second boat sink. What are the two forces acting on each boat? Are they balanced?

3 Fill in the shaded boxes. All the words have something to do with objects falling.

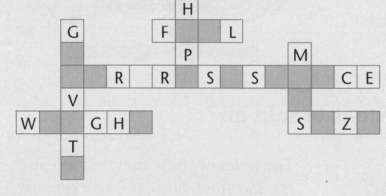

5 Here is a pan suspended on a spring. The spring stretches when an object is placed in the pan. Put the objects in order starting with the one that will stretch the spring the most.

packet of biscuits

5 kg potatoes

500 g cheese

packet of crisps

1 kg bag of flour

4 Can you explain these magic tricks? Write down in your own words what is happening and draw pictures to help you.

The magician marks a letter with a paper clip then spins the wheel and points his wand. The wheel stops when the marked letter is opposite the wand.

The magician points his wand at the toy boat and says 'Go, boat, go!' The boat moves in front of the wand and goes wherever the wand points.

Light and sound

Before you start you should know that:
- light comes from a variety of sources;
- the Sun is the greatest source of light for the Earth;
- the Moon is not a source of light but only reflects the light of the Sun;
- darkness is the absence of light;
- there are many kinds of sound;
- there are many sources of sound;
- sounds travel away from sources, getting fainter as they do so;
- sounds are heard when they enter the ear.

In this unit you will learn:
- that light travels in a straight line from its source;
- that mirrors can reflect light;
- about how we see things when light shines on them and is bounced off into our eyes;
- that light can pass through some materials but not through others;
- how shadows are formed when light cannot pass through an object;
- about how sounds are made when objects vibrate;
- that vibrations from sound sources can travel through some materials more easily than through others;
- how loud sounds can damage your ears;
- that the size of the vibrations affects the loudness of a sound;
- that fast vibrations make a high sound and slower vibrations make a lower sound.

Learning about light

Light travels in straight lines from its **source**. It cannot bend to travel around corners. Shiny surfaces, like a mirror, **reflect** light and make it travel in a different direction. We see things when light shines on them and is bounced off into our eyes.

How does light travel?

Light travels in straight lines from its **source**. It cannot bend round corners.

The children in Red class looked through straight tubes at a lighted candle. Everyone could see the candle. The light travels in straight lines in all directions from the candle.

The children tried looking through bendy tubes. No-one could see the candle. The light from the candle cannot travel around the bends in the tube.

How can light be made to travel round a corner?

Mina shone a torch at Jack. Jack **reflected** the light with a mirror so it shone back at Mina.

Jack turned the mirror to reflect the light on to the wall. The mirror makes the light travel in a different direction.

How do we see things?

You see objects when light shines on them. Light is bounced off an object and, when you look at it, the light enters your eyes.

If you look at an object in the dark you cannot see it because there is no light to bounce off it into your eyes.

Mina is reading a book. When the lamp is on she can see the page clearly.

Mina can only see the book when light is shining on it. The light is reflected (bounced off) the book into her eyes.

There is a power cut and the lamp goes out. Now Mina cannot see the book.

1 Copy the sentence and fill in the gaps. Light travels in a .... from its .... Mirrors can .... light.

2 Real darkness is where there is no light at all. Write down in your own words why we cannot see in the dark.

3 Draw yourself looking at a clock. Put in arrows to show how you see the clock. (Clue – Don't forget the source of light!)

Shadows

Shadows are made when light shines around an object but cannot shine through it. The shadow is made on the opposite side of the object from the light source. Shadows can be big or small. It depends on how far away the light source is from the object.

What makes a shadow?

A **shadow** is made when light shines on an object but cannot pass through the object. The object blocks the light so there is a dark shape behind the object where the light does not shine. This dark shape is the shadow.

When Jack shone a bright lamp on his teddy bear, a shadow appeared behind the bear.

The light from the lamp passes around the outside of the bear and makes a pool of light on the floor. The light cannot pass through the bear so the floor behind the bear stays dark.

Jack switched off the lamp and the teddy bear's shadow disappeared.

Where did the shadow go?

When light shines on an object from above, the object does not **cast** a shadow.

Jack noticed that the bear had no shadow. He lifted up the bear and saw the bear's shadow on the floor.

The **ceiling** light shines down on the bear and round the outside of it. The light still cannot shine through the bear so the shadow appears on the floor beneath the bear.

Why do shadows change in size?

Shadows get smaller as the distance between the object and the light source gets larger.

Jack sat the teddy bear near to a white wall and shone a bright lamp on the bear. The bear's shadow appeared on the wall behind it.

Jack moved his lamp further away from the bear. The bear's shadow got smaller.

When Jack moved his lamp close to the bear, the bear's shadow became very big.

---

1 Draw a picture and write down in your own words how shadows are formed.

2 Copy this sentence into your book and fill in the gaps.

When an object is close to a .... of light its shadow will be .... When an object is further away from a .... of light its shadow will be ....

Transparent, translucent and opaque

Light can shine through some materials but not others. **Opaque** materials will not let any light through. We can see through **transparent** materials, because they let all light through. **Translucent** materials let some light through but are not see-through.

Can you see through it?

Matthew held sheets of different materials up to the window. This is what he found out.

▼ *Translucent* materials

bubble wrap

fabric

greaseproof paper

These materials let light shine through but I can't see shapes clearly through them.

I can see clearly through these materials.

These materials let no light through at all and I can't see through them.

glass

cling film

perspex

wood

metal

foil

▲ *Transparent* materials

▲ *Opaque* materials

What materials make the best shadow puppets?

Matthew decided to make some shadow puppets from his
materials. He cut out some shapes and made a **screen** from
white paper. Light from a torch made the shadows.

He found out that the opaque materials made the best shadow
puppets because none of the light could get through. He cut
holes in some of the shapes to let the light through so that his
shadow puppets could have eyes, a nose and a mouth.

1 Look around your classroom. Draw
and label three things made from
transparent material, three things
made from opaque material and three
things made from translucent material.

2 Match the two halves of these
sentences correctly. Copy them
into your book.

■ Transparent materials let   no light through.
■ Opaque materials let   all light through.
■ Translucent materials let   some light through.

3 Which materials would you choose
to make a shadow puppet and why?
Write your sentence like this, filling in
the gaps.
I would choose .... and ....
.... because ....
....

Sound vibrations

Sound is made when a material **vibrates**. There are different ways of making **vibrations** to make sound. Fast vibrations make a high sound, slower vibrations make a lower sound. Large vibrations make a louder sound than small vibrations.

How do we make sound?

Sounds can be made by **plucking**, **blowing**, **shaking**, **beating** or **scraping instruments** or objects to make them **vibrate**.

How are high and low sounds made?

Fast **vibrations** make a high sound and slow vibrations make a low sound. Objects which vibrate many times every second make a **high-pitched** sound. Objects which vibrate only a few times every second make a very low sound.

As Yasmin blows into her **recorder** the air inside vibrates. When she covers up the holes there is more air inside to vibrate. The number of vibrations every second is fewer and the note sounds lower.

Daniel's bottle which has most water in it, vibrates slowly when tapped and makes a low note.

The same bottle makes a high-pitched sound when Daniel blows across the top of it.

How are loud and quiet sounds made?

Large vibrations make a loud sound. Small vibrations make a quiet sound. The drum skin vibrates when Jamal beats it. The sound echoes in the space inside the drum.

As Jamal beats the drum harder, the vibrations get bigger and the sound gets louder.

If you rub **sandpaper** blocks together, they vibrate and make a sound.

The harder you rub them together, the louder the sound becomes because the vibrations are bigger.

Jack makes a loud sound by shaking a tin that has pasta in it. The pasta and the tin vibrate as they bang together.

Jack makes a quieter sound by shaking a tin that has salt in it.

The salt grains are much smaller and cannot bang together as hard as the pasta. The vibrations are smaller so the sound is quieter.

1 Explain how materials vibrate to make:
   a   high sounds
   b   low sounds
   c   loud sounds
   d   quiet sounds

2 If Yasmin covers up just one hole on her recorder will it make a high note or a low note? What sort of note will it make if she covers up all the holes?

3 Predict what kind of sound Daniel could make if he tapped and blew over the bottle which has the least amount of water in it.

Sound can travel

Sound can travel through all materials but some materials carry sound better than others. Sound can travel through air but cannot travel through empty space. Hard materials can **reflect** sound so that the sound travels back in the opposite direction. This is called an **echo**.

How does sound travel?

Sound spreads out from its source like **ripples** spreading on a pond when a stone is dropped into it.

When sound hits a hard surface, it bounces back and travels in a new direction.

Sara could hear him clearly because the sound has been reflected off the walls and through the gap in the door.

▼ *Jason went outside the classroom door and called to Sara.*

Coo-ee, can you hear me?

Gosh! That means sound can travel round corners!

▼ *Jason closed the door and called again. Sara could still hear him but not as clearly as before.*

Hello!

▼ *Sara could still hear him because some sound travels through the door.*

So sound can travel through the door as well as round the corner!

Can sound travel through materials?

Jason sat with his ear pressed to the wooden table. Sara tapped a **tuning fork** and stood it on the other end of the table. The tuning fork vibrated and made a sound. Sara could hear it through the air. Jason could hear the sound quite loudly through the wooden table.

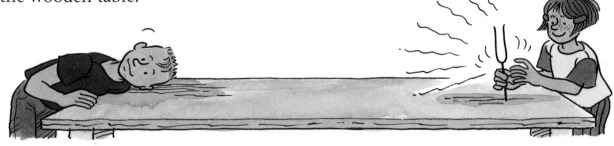

They covered the table with a thick cloth and tried again. Neither Sara nor Jason could hear a sound from the tuning fork. The hard wooden table carried the sound vibrations well but the soft cloth **absorbed** the vibrations so that no sound could be heard.

What makes an echo?

Jason and Sara were crossing the road using the **subway**. Sara ran on ahead. Jason called to her. His voice echoed round the subway.

The sound vibrations of Jason's voice hit the far end of the subway and bounced back. Jason and Sara heard the reflected sounds a little later.

Hard materials *reflect* sound but soft materials *absorb* sound. Echoes are made when sound bounces from one surface to another and back again.

1 Cowboys in old films put their ears to the ground to find out if Indians are coming. Write down why you think they do this.

2 Does the school hall echo more when it is full of children or empty? Try to explain why, in your own words.

Hearing sound

Sound can be heard when it enters our ears. Inside each ear is an **ear drum** which vibrates when sound vibrations hit it. Very loud sounds can damage the **delicate** parts inside our ears. We can use **ear muffs** to block out loud noise and protect our ears.

Can loud music damage your ears?

Michelle plays her music very loudly! Tom is not happy.

Michelle is wrong. Very loud music can damage your ears.

The shape of your **outer ear** helps to trap the sound and carry it into your ear. The important parts of your ear are inside your skull so they cannot be damaged easily.

Sound waves enter your ear and make the **ear drum** vibrate. Very loud music can damage the **delicate** parts inside your ear.

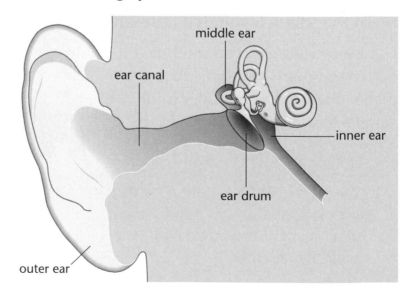

How can we block out sound?

Ear muffs **muffle** sound so that loud noise cannot reach the ear drum. Ear muffs cover up your ears. It is dangerous to push things inside your ear because it might damage the ear drum.

▲ *Sand bags also muffle sound.*

▲ *Heavy curtains absorb sound.*

Sound can pass through all materials including air. Soft materials like wool and cotton absorb sound waves.

1 Copy the diagram of the ear into your book. Label the part of the ear that vibrates when sound reaches it.

2 Which of these materials would make good ear muffs to block out sound?

wood   cotton   wool   solid plastic   sand   newspaper

Write a sentence about each of them like this.

I think wood is a .... material for ear muffs because ....
....
....

Test your knowledge

1 When Mina shines the torch at the mirror the light shines in Tom's eyes. Why? Copy the picture into your book and draw another arrow to show what is happening to the light. Write an explanation under the picture.

2 Copy the sentences and fill in the gaps using the words in the boxes and your own words to explain your choice.

I would use transparent glass for my .... because ....

I would use translucent glass for my .... because ....

I would use metal for my .... because it is .... and ....

garage door	kitchen window
bathroom window	opaque

3 Draw yourself and your shadow. (Don't forget the source of light!)

4 How do you play these instruments? Join the correct pairs.

guitar   beating
violin   blowing
trumpet   shaking
drum   plucking
maracas   scraping

5 What sort of vibrations produce a high, quiet sound? What sort of vibrations produce a low, loud sound?

6 When I visited Castle Dracula I went into three rooms. I was very frightened so I screamed a lot. Which room echoed my screams? Why?

■ The ballroom – a large empty room with velvet curtains and soft carpets.

■ The dungeon – a tiny room with dirty straw on the floor and rags hanging from the walls.

■ The kitchen – a large stone room that was completely empty.

Electricity

Before you start you should know:
- that many everyday appliances use electricity;
- how to construct simple circuits involving batteries, wires, bulbs and buzzers;
- that electrical devices will not work if there is a break in the circuit.

In this unit you will learn:
- how to make an electric circuit work;
- the difference between a battery and a cell;
- what is inside a light bulb;
- how a bulb works;
- what happens when buzzers and motors are used;
- that there are different types of electrical switches;
- how to make your models work;
- how to use electricity safely;
- about the dangers when working with electricity;
- what power stations, overhead cables, transformers and mains electricity do.

Making a circuit

A **bulb** lights when it is **connected** by wires to a **battery** in the right way. When the bulb is connected like this, we call it a **circuit**. The light from the bulb comes from a thin wire inside the lamp. This wire gets hot and glows when electricity passes through it.

What makes the bulb light?

To light a bulb you need the bulb, a **battery** and some wires. They must be **connected** the right way to make a **complete circuit**.

If you connect the wires to opposite ends of the battery the bulb will still light.

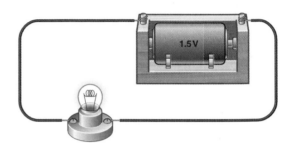

▼ *The circuit is complete – the bulb lights.*

What are the wires like?

The wires in the circuit are called either **leads** or **electrical cable**. Wires are made of metal.

▼ *This is a piece of electrical cable.*

metal core

plastic

Metals **conduct** electricity. They let electricity pass through. To make the wire safe to touch it is usually covered in plastic.

To make the bulb light *the metal wire* must touch the battery and the lamp connectors.

What happens if you remove the bulb?

Unscrew the bulb from its holder. The lamp will go out because no electricity is passing through the bulb.

Remove one of the leads from the battery. The same thing will happen – the bulb does not light.

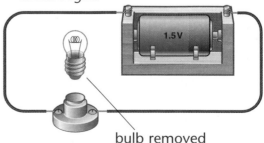

▼ *The circuit is not complete – the bulb doesn't light.*

bulb removed

What is inside the bulb?

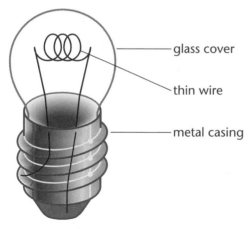

— glass cover

— thin wire

— metal casing

▲ *The wire gets hot and glows.*

Look closely at the bulb. You will see a thin wire inside the glass cover. The electricity must pass through this wire for it to get hot and give out light.

When the bulb is put in a circuit, one lead must touch the bottom of the bulb and the other lead must touch the metal **casing**.

Look carefully at this drawing. It shows you how to connect a bulb into a circuit without using a bulb holder.

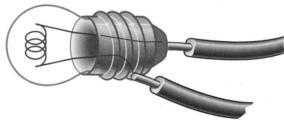

You can use leads made from *any wire*. As long as they are connected the right way to the battery, the bulb will light.

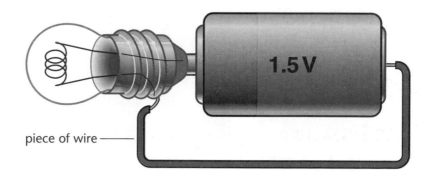

1.5 V

piece of wire ——

1 What part of the bulb lights up?

2 Make drawings of what you need to make a bulb light up.

3 Write down three good reasons why a bulb might not work when you fit it into a circuit.

4 Why is an electrical cable made of both metal and plastic?

Batteries

Batteries or **cells** provide the **voltage** to push electricity round a circuit. Batteries have **positive (+)** and **negative (–) terminals**. When a number of cells are used they must be connected positive to negative. The higher the voltage used, the brighter the bulb.

What do batteries do?

There are many different types of battery. **Torches** and some toys use the larger batteries. Watches and **calculators** use much smaller batteries. The **V** on the battery stands for **volts**. The **voltage** of the battery is the 'push' needed to make the electricity flow in the circuit.

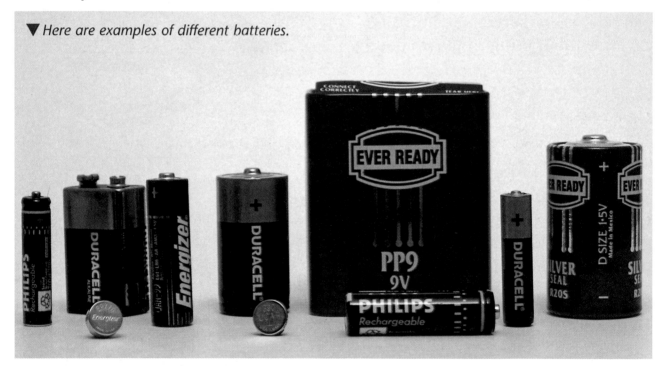

▼ *Here are examples of different batteries.*

The higher the voltage of a battery, the brighter the bulb will light when it is connected to the battery. A battery uses **chemicals** to make electricity. When these chemicals are used up, the battery stops working or goes 'flat'.

If you look carefully at a battery you will see that there is a plus sign (+) at one end and a minus sign (–) at the other. These ends are called the **terminals**. We write them as **positive** (+) and **negative** (–).

How do you connect a battery into a circuit?

Each 1.5 V battery is really called a **cell**. When you connect two or more cells together they are called **batteries**.

You must always connect the positive (+) terminal of one cell to the negative (−) terminal of another cell.

▲ *Connected like this cells will be able to work in a circuit.*

If you connect cells with two positive terminals touching, the circuit will not work. In the same way, a battery will not work if you connect two negative terminals together.

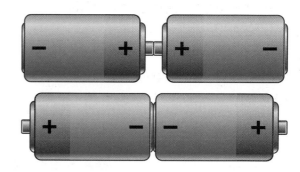

▲ *Neither of these will work in a circuit.*

A torch usually has more than one cell. The cells or batteries have to be connected in the same way – positive to negative – to light the bulb.

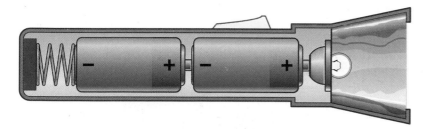

▲ *If you put the batteries in with both positive or both negative terminals touching, the torch bulb will not light.*

1 What is a cell?

2 What does a battery or cell do?

3 What happens to a battery if you use it in a circuit for a long time?

4 Make a drawing of the correct way to connect two cells.

5 Write down a list of everyday objects which use batteries.

Buzzers and motors

A **buzzer** in a circuit will make a noise. A **motor** in a circuit turns a wheel. Some buzzers work only if the electricity is flowing in one direction. If the flow is **reversed**, the buzzer does not work. Motors turn in the opposite direction when the flow of electricity is reversed.

Buzzers

A **buzzer** makes a noise when it is connected to a battery in a circuit. If you make a circuit with a battery, leads and a buzzer, you will hear the noise.

▼ *The buzzer makes a noise when the circuit is complete.*

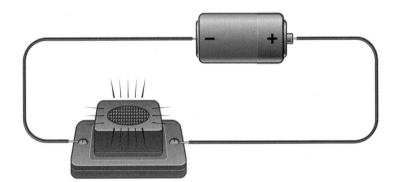

If you connect the leads to the opposite sides of the buzzer it may stop working. For some buzzers, the electricity can pass in only one direction.

Motors

If you connect a **motor** into the circuit you will be able to see the motor turning. Fit a coloured cardboard disc on to the motor and you will see the colours mixing together.

If you connect a bulb into this circuit, the wheel will not turn as fast.

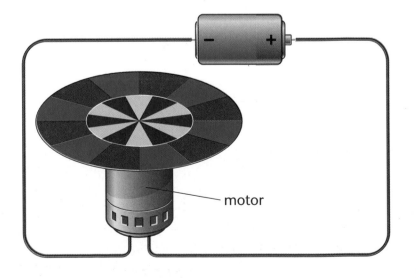

motor

How can we make the wheel change direction?

Look at this picture drawn on a cardboard **disc**. If you fit this disc on to the motor, you can see the motor changing direction. The leads must be connected to the battery and to the motor.

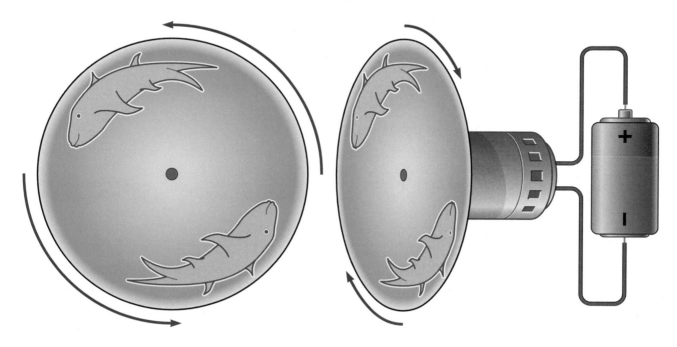

If you remove the leads from the battery and connect them to the opposite terminals, the motor will turn in the opposite direction. You will be able to see the fish swimming backwards.

Electricity flows from the positive terminal of the battery to the negative terminal. When you change the leads round, the electricity passes through the motor in the opposite direction. This makes the motor turn in the **reverse** direction.

1 What do you need to make a buzzer work?

2 How can you make a motor turn backwards?

3 Draw a picture of how you make two things work in a circuit, for example a lamp and a buzzer.

4 Mina was making her picture of a toy car turn on a disc attached to a motor. It was going too fast and she wanted to slow it down. Write down how she could do this or draw a picture.

Switches

• •

Switches are used to turn circuits or electrical **appliances** on or off. When a switch is closed or 'on' the circuit is complete. When a switch is open or 'off' the circuit is broken. All circuits need switches to stop the battery going flat.

• •

How can you make a simple switch?

Using a **switch** allows you to break a circuit.

You can make a simple switch by using a paper clip.	
The switch will work better if it can be connected to the ends of the leads more easily.	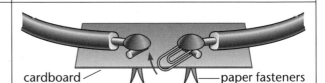
You can make a switch from metal foil, cardboard and two paper fasteners like this. You hold the cardboard closed to turn the switch on.	
Another switch which is easy to make uses a piece of springy metal like this.	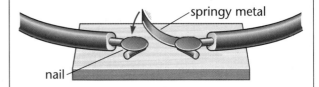

▼ *These are switches that you may find in your home.*

Can we find other ways of using switches?

Some **burglar alarms** work by sounding an alarm when a switch is pressed down and closed. They can be placed under a mat by the door so the alarm sounds as the burglar steps on to the mat.

Can we switch lights on and off separately?

Sara wanted 'stop' and 'go' lights for her train set. She needed to have a switch which would change the lights from green to red.

At first she tried using one switch. This made the lights come on and go off together.

She added a second switch between the red light and green light. Both lights still came on and went off together.

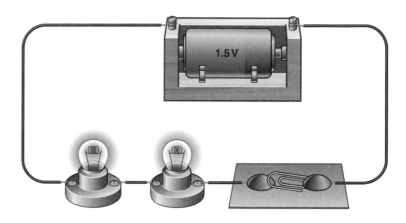

Sara then tried a new circuit. She had to move the paper clip from touching one lead to touching another. This time it worked. When the red light was on, the green light was off. When the green light was on, the red light was off.

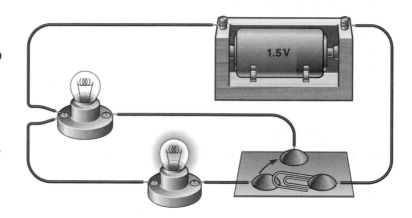

1 Why do you need a switch in a circuit?

2 Write down how you could make a simple type of switch or draw it.

3 Write down how a switch could be used to work a burglar alarm.

4 Invent your own type of switch. Draw a picture to show how your switch will work.

More circuits

Circuits can be used to make your **models** light up or work. It is important to use a battery with the correct voltage for the job it has to do. You can make a circuit which will do a number of different jobs.

Making your models work

Models can be made to work by fitting circuits inside. You always need a complete circuit and a switch. Without a switch you would run your battery down quickly.

The circuit inside the lighthouse makes its light turn on.

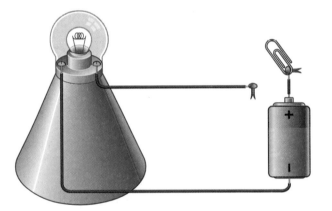

A motor fitted inside a model windmill will make the sails turn. It can work by **attaching** the motor to a **spindle** with an **elastic** band.

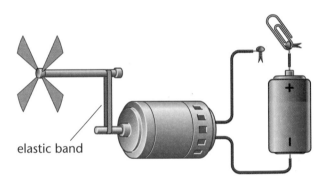

elastic band

Can we add more to a circuit?

You can add more parts into a circuit. In this one the clown's face has eyes and a shiny nose that light up. It also has a bow tie that spins.

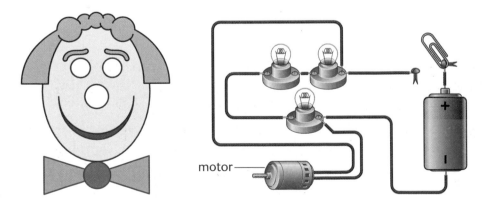

motor

Can you find a way to stop the bath from overflowing?

Daniel was often in trouble. He would turn on the water to run his bath and then forget about it. Water would overflow. He decided to make himself an alarm that would warn him when the bath was full.

This is how he solved the problem. He made a special type of switch and fitted this into a circuit with a buzzer. Daniel covered a plastic **float** with metal foil. Then he connected two pieces of metal foil to the leads in the circuit inside a large tube.

As the bath filled with water, the float rose. When the water was at the right level, the metal on the float touched the two pieces of metal. This completed the circuit. The buzzer sounded so that Daniel knew his bath was ready.

▼ *Daniel's water level checker.*

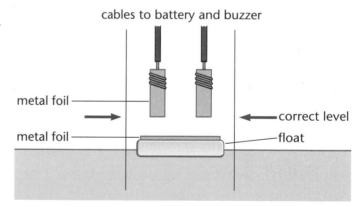

> **DANGER!**
> It is very dangerous to use mains electricity near water.
> **It can kill!**
> Daniel's circuit is only safe because he is using a battery with a low voltage.

1 Write down how to make a light turn on and off in a model house.

2 Draw the circuit you would use to make the wheels on a toy car turn.

3 Matthew and Mina wanted to put lights in the three rooms of their doll's house. They wanted to be able to switch them on and off separately. Draw the circuit they will need to use to do this.

103

Being safe with electricity

Overhead cables carry a very high voltage. Electricity in the home is 240 volts which is dangerous. If you touch any part which is bare metal when the electricity is turned on, you can get a serious electric shock. This might kill you.

Where does our electricity come from?

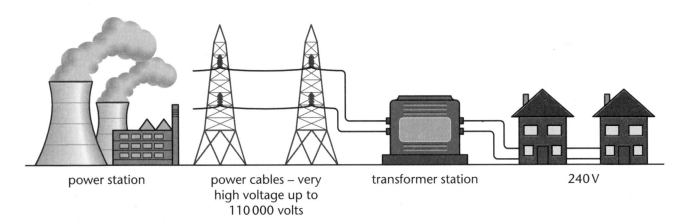

power station   power cables – very high voltage up to 110 000 volts   transformer station   240 V

Electricity is carried from **power stations** by cables to your home. You have probably heard that it is dangerous to fly a kite near **overhead cables**. The voltage is very high. The string of a kite could touch the cables and conduct the electricity through you.

In every town there are a number of small buildings called **transformer** stations. Here the electricity from the overhead cables is changed to a lower voltage for use in your home.

These buildings always have signs warning you to keep out as it is high-voltage electricity. Do not go near them.

Underground cables carry the electricity to your home. The voltage is now 240 volts but this is still dangerous. This is called **mains electricity**.

What dangers are there in your home?

The circuits you have made at school use only low voltages.
Your batteries are only about 3 volts. It is quite safe to touch
wires carrying 3 volts. Electric train sets run on 6 to 12 volts.
This is still fairly safe.

However, the voltage in the circuits in your home is 240 volts.
This is much higher and touching **live wires** can cause serious
injuries or death. Here is a picture of some dangers to avoid.

Can you spot *five* dangers in this picture?

1 Why are overhead cables dangerous?

2 What is the voltage of electricity in
your home?

3 What voltage does an electric train
set use?

4 Write down five things that are
dangerous to do near electricity.

5 Draw a poster which shows how to
use electricity safely.

Test your knowledge

1

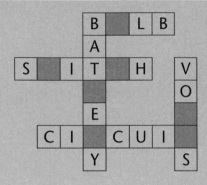

These words are all connected with electricity. Copy the crossword on to squared paper and fill in the blanks. Then write your own clues for these words.

2 Design a game that will teach young children how to be safe with electricity.

3 Match each statement to the correct word.

this turns when electricity flows through it	**switch**
this makes a noise when switched on	**motor**
this will turn a circuit on or off	**bulb**
a wire in this gets hot and gives out light	**buzzer**

4 Write these sentences in your book using words from the list to fill in the spaces.

The power of a battery is measured in .... The .... the voltage, the more work it can do. A bulb in a .... will be .... if a higher voltage .... is used.

battery, higher, brighter, volts, circuit

5 Which of these bulbs will work when connected into a complete circuit?

For each one, explain why it will or will not work.

A  **B**  **C**  **D**

The Earth and beyond

Before you start you should know:

- that light comes from a variety of sources, including the Sun;
- that darkness is the absence of light.

In this unit you will learn:

- about the sizes and shapes of the Earth, Moon and Sun;
- the positions of the Sun in the sky;
- how the Earth orbits the Sun;
- what makes day and night;
- that we can see only light sources and reflected light;
- about the sizes and positions of shadows during the day;
- what causes the seasons;
- how we see light from the Moon;
- why the shape of the Moon appears to change.

The Earth, the Sun and the Moon

The **Sun** is much bigger than the **Earth**. The Sun is a **star**. It is closer to the Earth than it is to other stars. The **Moon** is smaller than the Earth and closer than the Sun. The Moon **orbits** the Earth. The Earth, the Sun and the Moon are all round or ball-shaped.

What do we know about the Sun?

On clear days the **Sun** shines brightly in the sky. It is so bright because it is made from very hot gases. It looks small because it is a long way from us. In fact, it is very big, much bigger than **Earth**.

Earth

▲ *If the Earth was this size ...*

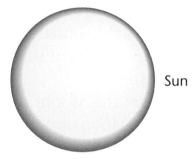

Sun

... the Sun would be ten times bigger than this.

▲ *Can you see this many stars on a clear night?*

On a clear night you can see lots of **stars**. They are just like our Sun but much further away. Our Sun is just one of the millions of stars.

Some stars are too far away to be seen clearly. You can only see these with **binoculars** or a **telescope**.

Galileo, who lived about 400 years ago, was the first **scientist** to study the Sun. He went blind from looking at it for too long. We now know it is very **dangerous** to look directly at the Sun.

All living things need light and heat from the Sun to grow.

What do we know about the Moon?

The **Moon** is moving in an **orbit** round the Earth. Sometimes we can see the Moon during the day if the sky is clear. At other times we see the Moon at night.

The Moon is easier to see at night because the sky is dark.

When you look at the Moon you will see it has dark patches on its surface. These are **craters** or huge holes up to 250 kilometres across.

The shape of the Earth, the Sun and the Moon

People used to believe that the Earth was flat. We now know that the Sun, the Moon and the Earth are all **spherical** like balls. **Astronauts** can see the shapes of the Earth and Moon from their **spacecraft**.

▲ *The Earth and Moon seen from space.*

1 Read the information about the Sun. Now write three sentences of facts about the Sun. Add more if you can.

2 Which is nearer to the Earth – the Sun or the Moon?

3 When can you see the Moon? Is it only at night-time?

4 Draw a diagram of what the Sun, the Moon and the Earth would look like seen from a **spaceship**.

Movements of the Sun

The Sun rises in the east and sets in the west. The Sun does not move but the Earth does. It spins like a top or turns on its own **axis**. The Earth completes one **rotation** every 24 hours. It also travels round the Sun taking a year to complete an orbit.

What happens to the Sun during the day?

When you get up in the morning, the Sun is in the east.

By midday the Sun is in the south but higher in the sky. In the evening the Sun sets in the west.

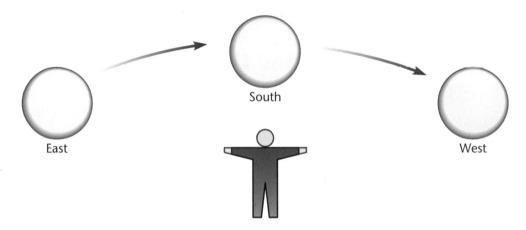

East

South

West

It seems that the Sun is moving around the Earth. For many years everyone believed that was what happened. Now we know that the Earth is moving, and not the Sun. The Earth is spinning like a top. Each day it turns a full **rotation**.

The Sun rises in the east as the Earth turns towards the Sun.

At midday the Sun will be facing you. In the evening the Sun sets in the west as the Earth turns away from the Sun into darkness.

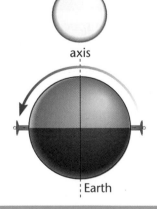

Sun

axis

Earth

What happens when the Sun sets?

As the Earth turns away from the Sun, the Sun disappears over the horizon. You may see some beautiful colours when the Sun is low in the sky.

How does the Earth move?

As well as turning on its own **axis**, the Earth is also moving round the Sun. It takes one year for it to complete a full cycle. The scientist, Sir Isaac Newton, explained how **gravity** holds the Earth in orbit round the Sun.

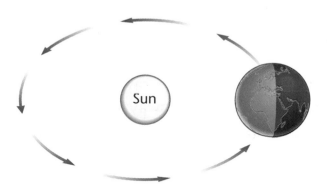

▲ *One orbit takes a year.*

1 From which direction does the Sun rise? In which direction does it set?

2 The Sun appears to be moving across the sky. Explain in your own words why this is not really what is happening.

3 How long does it take for the Earth to turn once on its axis?

4 How long does it take for the Earth to orbit the Sun?

Day and night

When the Sun lights up our part of the Earth it is our **daytime**. At night the Sun no longer shines on our part of the Earth. This will be our **night-time**. When it is our daytime it will be night-time on the opposite side of the Earth.

When do we have daytime?

When the Sun rises, light falls on our part of the Earth. This is our **daytime**. As the Earth turns, the Sun continues to light up the sky. When it is dull the Sun's rays still spread light through the clouds.

person in daylight

▲ It will be daylight for the part of the Earth facing the Sun.

As the Sun sets the sky will get darker. Even when the Sun can no longer be seen, its rays continue to light up the sky. As the Earth turns further away from the Sun, the sky becomes dark. While it is **night-time** in our part of the Earth, it will be daylight on the other side of the Earth.

person in the night

▲ It will be night-time for the part of the Earth facing away from the Sun.

At night-time no light from the Sun reaches us. Darkness is the **absence** of light.

What can we see at night?

At night we can see only things that give out light. This may be from light **sources** such as street lighting or lights from buildings.

Some cities like Hong Kong have many lights which make them bright at night.

We can also see some objects because they **reflect** light. This means that when light falls on an object it passes the light back so that we can see it.

Light coloured objects reflect better than dark objects. Some of the buildings in this photograph of Athens show up because they are reflecting light.

Can cats see in the dark?

People say that cats can see in the dark. This is not true. If there is no light they will not be able to see anything. However, cats do have very good **eyesight** and can see things in much **dimmer** light than we can.

1 What causes daytime? Try to explain it in your own words.

2 What happens when it becomes dark?

3 Make a list of things that can be seen at night. Try to divide them into two groups – things that are light sources and things that reflect light.

4 After dark, roads are more dangerous. How can they be made more safe for walkers, cyclists and cars?

Shadows through the day

As the Sun crosses the sky, the **shadows** move round. Shadows are longer in the mornings and evenings than at midday. They are at their shortest at midday. Shadows form when the light from the Sun is shaded by an object.

What makes a shadow?

If you stand outside on a sunny day you will see your **shadow**. When you move so will your shadow. Your shadow will always be on the side that faces away from the Sun.

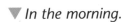
▼ *In the morning.*

▼ *At midday.*

Matthew went into the playground in the morning and then again at midday. He found the length of his shadow had changed. In the morning it was longer than at midday.

In the morning and in the afternoon the Sun is lower in the sky than at midday. The higher the Sun in the sky, the shorter the shadow. By the evening Matthew found that his shadow had become very long.

What happens to shadows throughout the day?

Matthew and Yasmin decided they would find out more about shadows. Matthew drew round Yasmin's shadow at different times during a sunny day.

They found that as the Sun appeared to move from east to west, the position of the shadow changed. The shadow became shorter as the Sun rose higher in the sky. As the Sun sank lower in the sky, Yasmin's shadow became longer.

Matthew and Yasmin cast shadows because they are both **opaque**. Light cannot pass through them. A shadow is formed when their bodies prevent light from reaching the ground.

▲ We can use shadows on a sun-dial to tell the time.

1 What differences are there between a shadow at midday and a shadow in the morning?

2 What causes a shadow to form?

3 Sara is sitting on a beach under a sunshade. During the day she has to keep moving to stay in the shade. Draw pictures of the sunshade and its shadows to show how they will change during the day.

The seasons

In Britain there are four **seasons** – spring, summer, autumn and winter. The days are short in winter and long in summer. When the days are long, there is more time for the Sun's heat to warm the Earth. When the nights are long, the Earth has more time to cool.

What changes occur in the seasons?

Have you noticed how the weather changes during the year? Most living things change with the **seasons**. A tree produces leaves and flowers in the spring. By the summer the tree has lots of leaves which fall in the autumn. In winter the branches are bare.

You will see from these pictures that the Sun is higher in the sky in summer than in winter. That part of the Earth will be warmer in summer than in winter. This also means the shadows are shorter in summer than in winter.

Many animals change during the winter. Animals like sheep and dogs grow thicker fur to keep them warm. Some small animals **hibernate**. Many animals give birth to their young in the spring so that they can grow while there is plenty of food.

What happens to the day length?

In summer the days are much longer than in winter. It gets light early in the morning and does not get dark until late. In the winter the opposite happens. The days are short and the nights are much longer.

▲ *People in Britain need to wear warm clothes in winter.*

▲ *A hot summer's day.*

The Sun has less time to heat up the Earth in winter than in summer. The long nights give more time for the Earth to cool down. So winter temperatures are lower than summer temperatures.

In the summer the Sun has longer to heat up the Earth than in winter. The short nights give less time for the Earth to cool down. So summer temperatures are higher than winter temperatures.

What happens in other parts of the world?

While it is winter in Britain, it is summer in the southern half of the world. When it is summer in Britain, it is winter in **Australia** and **South Africa**. In **tropical** countries the day length is the same all year. They do not have seasons. It is always warm.

1 Describe the weather in Britain in the four seasons.

2 How does the day length change during the year?

3 Why does the length of day cause the temperature to change?

4 How are the seasons in Australia different from seasons in Britain?

The Moon

The Moon is moving round the Earth. It takes 28 days to complete one cycle. The Moon reflects light from the Sun. The shape of the Moon appears to change. This depends on how much of the sunlit surface we see.

What do we know about the Moon's movements?

The Moon is in orbit round the Earth. It takes 28 days for the Moon to orbit the Earth. Our word 'month' comes from the word 'moon'.

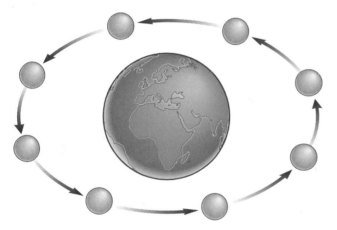

▲ It takes 28 days for the Moon to orbit the Earth.

The Moon also turns on its own axis once every 28 days. This means that the same side of the Moon always faces Earth.

We found out what the other side was like only when spacecraft travelled round the Moon. As scientists had expected, it is much the same as the side we can see.

Does the Moon shine?

The Moon is not like a star. It is made from rocks, not hot gases. It is not like the Sun giving out heat and light. It only *appears* to shine because it is *reflecting* light from the Sun.

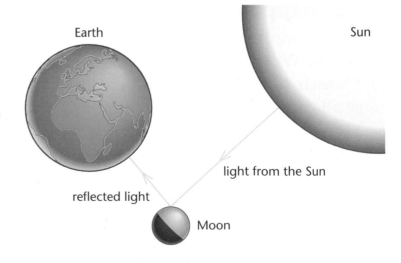

Earth

Sun

light from the Sun

reflected light

Moon

Why does the Moon appear to change shape?

You may have noticed that sometimes the Moon looks **circular**. This is a **full moon**. At other times it may be a **half moon** or a **crescent**. Its shape depends on how much of its surface we see lit by the Sun.

For part of the month the Moon cannot be seen from Earth. This is when the Moon is between the Earth and the Sun. This is called a **new moon**.

Jack decided he would keep a diary of the shape of the Moon for four weeks. Each day he looked for the Moon and drew a picture of its shape.

He found that during the four weeks its shape changed from a new moon to a crescent, then to a half moon, then to a full moon and back again.

| Day 1 new moon | Day 3 crescent | Day 7 half moon | Day 15 full moon | Day 21 half moon | Day 24 crescent | Day 28 new moon |

Jack found that each month the Moon goes through a cycle when its shape appears to change. We call these the **phases** of the Moon.

If you watch the Moon for a day you will find that, like the Sun, it rises in the east and sets in the west.

1 If you were on the Moon what would it look like?

2 How long does it take for the Moon to orbit the Earth?

3 From which direction does the Moon rise and where does it set?

4 Explain in your own words why the Moon's shape appears to change during the month.

5 How does the Moon shine?

Test your knowledge

1 Choose the correct words from the list to complete each sentence. Write out each one in your book.

   a The Moon rises in the .... **north, south, east, west**

   b When our part of the Earth faces away from the Sun, it will be our .... **daytime, night-time**

   c A shadow is shortest at .... **morning, midday, evening**

2 Look at the picture. What season do you think it is? What clues can you find in the picture?

3 Place these in order of size from biggest to smallest:

   Earth   school   Britain

   England   adult   child   Sun

   Moon   town   house

4 These words are all from this unit but they have been mixed up.

   Write down the correct words in your book.

   wasdoh   onmo   nus   taher

   nsaoes   rtsa   suisren

5 For each of these sentences decide whether it is true or false.

   ■ Sometimes you can see the Moon in the daytime.
   ■ The Sun is in orbit round the Earth.
   ■ All countries have spring, summer, autumn and winter but at different times of the year.
   ■ During the day the stars are on the other side of the Earth.
   ■ You can damage your eyesight if you look at the Sun.
   ■ In the morning the Sun is lower in the sky than at midday.

   Make a list of the 'true' sentences and a list of the 'false' sentences.

   Try to change the false sentences to make them true.

Glossary

Humans and other animals

birds   Living things which have wings and lay eggs.

bones   The parts of an animal's body which make up the skeleton.

canines   Pointed teeth used for holding and tearing food.

carnivores   Animals that eat meat.

classify   Arrange or sort living things into similar groups.

decay   The rotting down of animals or plants after they die.

fish   Living animals which have gills and fins.

herbivores   Animals that eat plants.

hinge joint   Joint which will only bend one way, like a door hinge, such as knee, elbow and finger joints.

incisors   Sharp teeth used for biting food.

insects   Living animals, like bees and dragon flies, which have three body parts and six legs.

life cycle   A diagram which shows the important stages in a plant or an animal's life.

mammals   Living animals which have live babies and make milk to feed their young, such as cows and humans.

milk teeth   First set of human teeth that come out as permanent teeth grow.

molars   Teeth with flat tops used for grinding food.

muscles   Fleshy parts of the body, joined to bones to make them move.

omnivores   Animals that eat meat and plants.

permanent teeth   Second set of human teeth, that form underneath milk teeth and push them out as they grow.

predators   Animals that eat other animals.

prey   Animals that are eaten by other animals, such as birds are eaten by foxes, mice are eaten by owls.

producers   Green plants which use energy from the Sun to make their food so they can grow and reproduce.

reproduce   To make young ones.

skeleton   The collection of bones which hold the body together and allow it to move.

Living things

adapted   A plant or animal which is suited to survive in its normal habitat.

bush   A woody plant which is smaller than a tree.

dispersal   The way seeds are spread away from their parent plant.

environment   A place where animals and plants live because of the conditions there.

ferns   Plants which have leaves which unfold from a spiral and carry spores underneath them.

flowering plants   Plants that have flowers.

flowers   The part of a plant where reproduction takes place.

fruit   These contain the seed or seeds of a plant.

germination   When seeds first start to grow and produce tiny roots and shoots.

grass   A plant with long thin leaves and flowers without any bright coloured petals.

habitat   A place where a plant or animal lives.

leaves   The part of a plant which collects sunlight, water and carbon dioxide and uses these to make the food for the plant.

moss   Very small plants which have spores that are made in swollen sacs called capsules.

roots   The part of a plant, normally below the surface, which helps keep it firmly in place and take water and minerals from the soil into the plant.

scattered   Spread out, or dispersed in every direction.

seedling   A baby plant, or a plant which has just germinated with a few leaves and roots.

species   Animals or plants which look very like each other.

stems   The main body or stalk of a plant.

tree   A large plant with a woody stem or trunk.

Materials and their properties

absorbent material   A material which is able to take in and hold liquid.

chalk   A white soft rock often found in soil.

clay   Very fine particles, often found in soil.

conductor   Material that allows heat to pass through easily.

drainage   When a liquid passes between solid particles.

dull   A property of material. Does not reflect light.

fabric   Manufactured cloth.

flexible   Able to bend easily without breaking.

gas   One of the three states of materials. Gas is spread out to fill all available spaces. Water vapour is the gas state of water.

insulate   To cover something to keep it hot or cold for longer.

liquid   One of the three states of materials. Liquids pour and spread out to take the shape of the container.

manufactured   Made by humans. When a raw material, such as wood, is changed into a new material, such as paper, it has different properties.

mineral   A substance which is taken out of the ground.

mixture   A combination of two or more different materials which can be separated out again.

moulded   Made into a new shape.

nitrogen   A colourless gas that makes up 78% of the air.

oxygen   A colourless gas, needed for breathing, which makes up 21% of the air.

particle   A very small piece of a substance.

property   A characteristic of a material.

sand   Small rounded grains of rock.

shiny   A property of material. Reflects light.

sieve   To separate a mixture of different sized solid particles by passing them through mesh.

soil   Natural material made when rocks are worn away. Contains different sized particles of rock and animal and plant matter.

solid   One of the three states of materials. Solids keep their shape unless a force is applied.

thermal insulator   A material which does not allow heat to pass through easily.

transparency   The property of letting light through. Glass is transparent.

Changes in materials

Celsius   A scale used to measure temperature.

chemically changed   When a reaction occurs to form a new substance.

coarse   Materials which contain particles of different sizes and feel gritty.

dissolve   To mix solid particles with liquid so that the solid becomes part of the liquid.

evaporation   When a liquid turns into a gas.

filter   To separate insoluble substances from a liquid by passing the liquid through a material which will not allow the solids to pass through.

filter paper   A special paper used in filtering. The paper will let water or other liquids pass through but will keep solid particles back.

fine   Small. For example, fine flour has small particles.

freeze   To change from a liquid to a solid.

ice   The solid form of water.

insoluble   Will not dissolve.

irreversible change   A change of state of materials where the materials cannot be changed back to their original state.

melt   To change from a solid to a liquid state.

ovenproof   A material which can stand the heat of an oven, and will not crack, melt or change its shape when very hot.

powder   A solid which contains small dry particles.

reversible change   A change of state of materials where the materials can be returned to their original state.

saturated solution   A mixture of soluble solids and liquid where the liquid is unable to dissolve any more of the solid.

solubility   The process of being soluble.

soluble   Can dissolve in liquid.

suspension   Tiny solid particles that are spread out in a liquid but not dissolved.

temperature   A measure of heat energy, or how hot or cold something is.

thermometer   An instrument with which to measure temperature.

water vapour   The gas state of water.

zero degrees Celsius (0 °C)   The temperature at which water freezes.

All about forces

air resistance   The force that the air exerts on a moving object.

attract   To pull towards each other.

balanced   When two forces of the same size act in opposite directions.

elastic   A flexible material which is able to stretch and go back to its original shape or length after it is pulled.

exert   To cause *something* to act upon *something else*.

float   To be supported by water. The downward force of gravity and the upthrust of the water are equal.

force   A push, pull, twist or turn.

gravity   The force that causes all objects to fall towards the centre of the Earth.

magnet   An object made from iron, nickel or cobalt materials which attracts other objects made from these materials.

magnetic   Able to be attracted by a magnet.

mass   The amount of matter in an object, measured in grams (g).

opposite   Exactly different from something else in every way.

poles   The ends of a magnet which exert a magnetic force.

pull   To give an object a force and make it move towards you.

push   To give an object a force and make it move away from you.

repel   To push away from each other.

similar   The same as something else.

sink   To fall to Earth in water. The downward force of gravity is greater than the upthrust of the water.

speed   How fast an object is travelling.

squash   To make something shorter by pushing it from opposite directions.

stationary   Not moving at all.

stretch   To make something longer by pulling it from opposite directions.

turn   Circular movement.

twist   Two forces acting on an object to make it turn.

unbalanced   When two forces of different sizes act in different directions.

weight   The downward force exerted on an object by gravity.

Light and sound

absorb   To take in or to reduce the effect of something.

beating   Striking with an instrument such as a stick or a hammer.

blowing   Pushing air into something with your mouth.

ear   Part of your body which detects sound.

echo   The reflection of sound by a hard surface.

light   A form of energy. The glow produced by something when it is very hot.

loud   A very noisy sound.

mirror   An object with a highly polished surface which reflects light. When you look in a flat mirror you see an image of yourself.

opaque   Not see-through. Lets no light through at all.

plucking   Pulling sharply on a string with your finger then letting go immediately.

quiet   A sound which you can hardly hear at all.

reflect   To bounce back from a surface in the opposite direction.

scraping   Rubbing one material across another material.

shadow   The dark area which forms on the opposite side of an object from the light source when light cannot pass through the object.

shaking   Moving something rapidly from side to side in the air using your hands.

sound   A form of energy which is caused by vibrations.

sound wave   The way sound travels from its source in a circular movement, spreading out like ripples in water.

source   The place where something begins.

translucent   Not see-through. Lets some light through.

transparent   See-through. Lets all light pass through.

vibrate   To move repeatedly with small regular movements.

vibration   Repeated small regular movements.

Electricity

appliance   A household device which uses electricity. Cookers and washing machines are electrical appliances.

battery   This provides the power which causes electricity to flow in the circuit. It is made of two or more cells.

bulb   An electrical component which lights up when it is placed in a circuit. A thin wire inside gets hot and glows.

buzzer   An electrical component which buzzes when electricity flows through it.

cell   A device which changes energy stored in chemicals into electrical energy. A battery is made of two or more cells joined together.

circuit   Components joined together by wires make a circuit. Electricity can flow round the circuit.

conduct   When materials allow electricity to flow. Metals are good conductors, plastic and rubber are not.

leads   The wires used to connect the different parts (components) of an electrical circuit together.

live wires   Wires which are connected to the mains electricity. They can give you a powerful shock or even kill you.

mains electricity   Electricity which is supplied to and used in the home.

motor   An electrical component which allows a wheel to rotate when electricity flows through it.

overhead cable   Wires that carry electricity which has a lot of energy (high voltage) over long distances.

power station   A building which has special machines to produce electricity from fuels and send it out to our homes, shops and factories.

switch   A device used in a circuit. When it is 'off' it stops the electricity flowing. When it is 'on' the circuit will be complete.

terminals   The parts of a battery to which the leads must be connected in a circuit.

transformer   A device which changes the amount of energy which is carried by electricity. Often they change high voltage electricity (in which a lot of energy is carried) to a lower voltage (in which less energy is carried).

voltage   The power needed to push electricity round the circuit.

volts   The units for measuring the power of a cell or battery. Cells are 1.5 volts. Batteries are 3 volts or more.

The Earth and beyond

craters   Very large holes found on the Moon's surface. Some are also found on Earth.

crescent   The way the Moon looks when it looks curved and only about one quarter of it is lit up.

daytime   The time when the Sun lights up our side of the Earth.

Earth   The planet on which we live.

Earth's axis   An imaginary line drawn through the centre of the Earth from the North to the South pole around which the Earth spins.

full moon   The way the Moon looks when it is fully lit up.

half moon   The way the Moon looks when it is only half lit up.

Moon   A satellite in orbit around Earth. It is made from rocks which reflect light from the Sun.

new moon   The way the Moon looks when it is not lit up at all.

night-time   The time when our part of the Earth is turned away from the Sun.

orbit   The curved path of an object like a planet around the Sun or the path of the Moon around the Earth.

reflect   To pass back light from a surface so that it can be seen.

rotation   Revolving around an axis: the Earth rotates (spins) around its axis.

seasons   Our spring, summer, autumn and winter. They are caused by a change in temperature and daylength during the year.

shadow   The dark area which forms on the side of an object which is shaded from light.

spherical   Shaped like a sphere or a ball.

stars   Very large objects in space. These are long distances away. They are made from very hot gases and give out light.

Sun   This is the nearest star to Earth and gives out heat and light. The Earth orbits the Sun.